S0-AFV-756

Vision 2020

What does the future hold?
Vision 2020 asks top business people
to look forward to the challenges and threats
that the dramatically altered landscape
of the future presents.

Every spectrum of the business sector is represented —
banking, the arts, agriculture, education, manufacturing,
government, trade unions, science and tourism. The result
is an informed — and fascinating — vision of business up to
the year 2020.

Vision 2020
What Future for Business?

Edited by
Liam Connellan

THE O'BRIEN PRESS
in association with
THE ROYAL DUBLIN SOCIETY
DUBLIN

First published 1995 by The O'Brien Press Ltd., 20 Victoria Road, Rathgar, Dublin 6.

01 02 03 04 05 06 07 08 09 10
95 96 97 98 99 00 01 02 03 04

British Cataloguing in Publication Data
Vision 2020: What Future for Business?
I. Connellan, Liam
338.0905
ISBN 0-86278-426-3
Typesetting, layout and design: The O'Brien Press, Dublin
Cover design: Slick Fish Design, Dublin
Printing: Colour Books Ltd, Baldoyle, Dublin

CONTENTS

Liam Connellan is vice president of the RDS – the Royal Dublin Society - and was chairman of the RDS Industry Committee 1991-94. He is also chairman of the National Roads Authority, of Generale des Eaux Ireland, and of the Smurfit Job Creation Enterprise Fund. He is a director of Johnson & Higgins, a member of the Board of Governors and Guardians of the National Gallery of Ireland, of the Economic and Social Committee of the European Union, and of the European Commission High Level Expert Group on the Societal Impact of Information Technology. President of the German Irish Chamber of Industry and Commerce, Liam Connellan was awarded the Cross of Merit (First Class) of the Federal Republic of Germany. He is president of the Irish Swedish Business Association and, from 1972 to 1992, was director general of the CII – the Confederation of Irish Industry.

ABOUT THE CONTRIBUTORS

James P Culliton is currently chairman of the Allied Irish Bank group (AIB), Ireland's largest banking and financial services group which has a strong international presence. The group operates mainly in Ireland and the United Kingdom, and through its wholly-owned subsidiary, First Maryland Bankcorp, in the United States. He is also chairman of Unidare plc and Northern Telecom (Ireland) Ltd, deputy chairman of Hibernian Group plc and director of a number of other companies. In 1992, he chaired the Review Body on Industrial Policy for the Government which produced the influential Culliton Report. For thirteen years James Culliton served as chief executive of CRH plc (Cement Roadstone Holdings) from 1974 to 1987. He is a former president of the MII – the Marketing Institute of Ireland, and a former chairman of the RTE Authority. He also served for a number of years on the board of IDA Ireland – the Industrial Development Authority, and on the executive committee of CII. He was awarded the RDS Industry Gold Medal in 1994 in recognition of his exceptional contribution to industry in Ireland.

Eddie O'Connor is managing director of Bord na Móna, the national peat company with subsidiaries in the UK, France and the US. Appointed in 1987, Dr O'Connor initiated a transformational programme through which the company was decentralised. Research and development and engineering functions were improved, and a new generation of machinery and an innovative method of production were introduced. In recognition of his work at Bord na Móna, the International Management Centres Europe awarded him an honorary doctorate in 1991. Prior to joining Bord na Móna, Dr O'Connor was fuel purchasing manager at the ESB – the national Electricity Supply Board, where he developed a maintenance planning system which became a world standard. Dr O'Connor is a member of the executive and council of the IMI – the Irish Management Institute, and a member of the board of the Institute of Directors.

Senator Feargal Quinn is managing director of Superquinn, the Irish supermarket group which he founded in 1960 and which has an international reputation for excellence in customer service. He is known for canvassing and responding directly to customers' needs, and credits them with many of the innovations that Superquinn has pioneered. These include children's playhouses at each of his sixteen supermarkets.

Feargal Quinn is a board member of a number of international retailing organisations, and has received several honorary degrees and other awards. He was chairman of the Irish post office for ten years from 1979 to 1989. He is author of the book *Crowning the Customer* which has been published in Ireland, America, Finland and Sweden, and translated into French, Dutch and Spanish. He was elected to the Irish Senate in 1993 as an independent member. He received the papal knighthood, Knight of St Gregory, in 1994.

Ciarán Benson is chairman of the Arts Council (1993-1998) and is a professor of psychology and head of department in University College Dublin. His academic interests include questions in aesthetics and theory of self. He was a founder member and past chairman of both the Irish Film Institute and the City Arts Centre, Dublin. His contributions to questions of cultural policy include *The Place of the Arts in Irish Education* (Dublin: The Arts Council, 1979) and *Art and the Ordinary* (Dublin: The Arts Council and Gulbenkian Foundation, 1989). His most recent publication was called *The*

Absorbed Self: Pragmatism, Psychology and Aesthetic Experience (London: Harvester Wheatsheaf, 1993). Under his chairmanship the Arts Council developed and presented the Arts Plan 1995-1997 to government in 1994.

David Kingston has been managing director of Irish Life plc, one of the leading life assurance companies in Europe with assets of over £6,500 million, since 1984. Through its subsidiaries, Irish Life has interests in general insurance, mortgage funding and banking. Irish Life transacts all forms of life assurance, group pension schemes, group life assurance schemes, pensions for the self-employed, annuities and investment savings. He holds a degree in mathematics from Oxford University. He is a Fellow of the Pensions Management Institute, and an Associate of the Society of Investment Analysts. He was president of the Society of Actuaries in Ireland from 1983 to 1985; president of the Irish Insurance Federation from 1987 to 1988; chairman of the Financial Services Industry Association from 1990 to 1994; and a member of the council of the Faculty of Actuaries from 1987 to 1990.

Brian N Sweeney is chairman and managing director of Siemens Ltd, chairman of Siemens Nixdorf Information Systems Ltd and Software and Systems Engineering Ltd, and board member of ESB Industrial Holdings Ltd, the Enterprise Trust and the National Technological Park, Plassey, as well as executive council member of IBEC – the Irish Business and Employers Confederation – and a member of the council of the NESC – National Economic and Social Council.
Previously he held the post of president of The Institution of Engineers in Ireland, the MBA Association and was a former chairman and president of the German Irish Chamber of Industry and Commerce. He was twice decorated by the President of the Federal Republic of Germany for support of German/Irish bilateral industrial and commercial relations – the Great Officers Cross of Merit with Ribbon, and Cross of Merit (First Class).

Pádraig O hUiginn is currently chairman of Bord Fáilte, the Irish tourist authority. From 1982 he was Secretary of the Department of the Taoiseach. He has been chairman of the National Economic and Social Council since 1984. In addition, he has chaired the Central Review Committee, the representative of government and the social partners, which oversaw the development of the Programme for Economic and Social Progress. Since 1987 he has been chairman of the International Financial Services Committee. He was also chairman of the Task Force on Employment and the Task Force on Tourism whose recommendations have been incorporated in the Programme for a Partnership Government 1993-1997. He has also served in the departments of the Environment, Industry and Commerce, Lands and Economic Planning and Development, and has extensive international experience at senior levels.

John F Daly has been responsible for the development of ICL Computers in Ireland for the past twenty-five years, first as chief executive and, since 1993, as chairman. He is the immediate past-president of the Dublin Chamber of Commerce where he was responsible for establishing the 2010 Committee which will identify the priorities which must be addressed to ensure an optimum future for the capital.

In addition John Daly is also a member of the Dublin Port and Docks Board, a member of the Advisory Committee of the National Treasury Management Agency and has a number of other business interests.

Tom Byrnes lectures in Strategic Management at the Michael Smurfit Graduate School of Business University College Dublin. Prior to joining the Faculty of Commerce he was part-owner, president and chief operating officer of an interexchange carrier in the mid-western United States. In 1985 he became group executive for corporate planning and information systems for the Jefferson Smurfit group, an integrated manufacturer and converter of paper and board with a large number of subsidiary and associated undertakings worldwide. Before that he was chief executive officer of Telecom Eireann, the Irish national telephone company, and also of IBM Ireland.

Dr Dervilla M X Donnelly is professor of organic chemistry (phytochemistry) at University College Dublin. She is also chairman of the Custom House Docks Development Authority. The Authority is working to secure the redevelopment of the Custom House Docks Area where the International Financial Services Centre is based.

In addition Dr Donnelly is executive council member and vice president of the European Science Foundation, a Fellow of the Royal Society of Chemistry and president of the Institute of Chemistry of Ireland. Recently elected vice president of ESTA – the European Science and Technology Assembly, she is also a member of the Royal Irish Academy and was the first woman president of the Royal Dublin Society.

Tony Barry was appointed chairman of CRH plc – Cement Roadstone Holdings – a multinational corporation involved in manufacturing products for use in the construction industry, in 1994. His career with CRH began in 1964 and he served as managing director of subsidiary and groups of subsidiary companies from 1972. He was appointed to the board of directors in 1978 and became chief executive of the group in 1988. Tony Barry is also a director of Greencore plc, a director of the Court of the Bank of Ireland, and of DCC – the Development Capital Corporation. He is senior vice president of the Irish Business and Employers Confederation. A member of The Institution of Civil Engineers, London, he is also a Fellow of The Institution of Engineers of Ireland.

John Dunne was appointed the first director general of the Irish Business and Employers Confederation on its establishment in January 1993. He has represented Irish companies at a range of different levels and has been involved in central negotiations with the government and the trades unions for many years, most notably in the PESP (Programme for Economic and Social Progress), the PNR (Programme for National Recovery) and the PCW (Programme for Competitiveness and Work). John Dunne is also a member of the National Economic and Social Council, the Central Review Committee, the executive committee of UNICE – the Confederation of European Industry and Employers Organisations – and a number of other bodies.

William Attley is General Secretary of SIPTU, Ireland's largest union, representing services, industrial, professional and technical staff. SIPTU is a national organisation with offices in every county and also in Northern Ireland. Bill Attley played a vital role in the amalgamation of the former ITGWU (the Irish Transport and General Workers Union) and the FWUI (the Federated Workers Union of Ireland) with the former SIPTU, and is also widely regarded as one of the key architects of the social partnership approach to the management of the economy.

He is an executive council member of the Irish Congress of Trade Unions

(ICTU). He is a member of the board of FÁS – the industrial training authority; An Bord Tráchtála – the Irish Trade Board; the National College of Industrial Relations; the Institute of European Affairs; and of the Radio Telefís Eireann Authority. He is a member of the Economic and Social Committee of the European Union, and of the Economic Committee of ETUC – the European Trade Union Confederation.

Matthew Dempsey is chief executive of the *Irish Farmers Journal* which had a weekly circulation in excess of 71,000 in 1994. He has been editor of the *Journal* since 1988, a position which he retains. He was chairman of the Agricultural Institute from 1985 to 1988, and chairman of ACOT – the National Agricultural Advisory and Education Service, from 1986 to 1988. He is also a member of the council of the Royal Dublin Society. He was producer of agricultural programmes at RTE radio for some years and presented a weekly radio programme from 1979-1987. From 1973 to 1987 he was EEC correspondent for the *Irish Farmers Journal*. He has also farmed extensively in Co Kildare.

Patrick O'Neill has been group managing director of Avonmore Foods plc since 1984. Avonmore Foods plc activities comprise the processing and marketing of dairy and food products including liquid milk, fresh milk products and meat products, and the manufacture of animal feedstuffs. In addition, he is a director of the Avonmore group, Forbairt, the Irish Permanent Building Society, the Irish Co-op Petroleum, and Norish (Kilkenny) Ltd, and he is president of the Irish Quality Association. He was chairman of the Pigs and Bacon Commission 1977-84; chairman of CBF - the Irish Livestock and Meat Board 1982-84; and chairman of Dublin City University Educational Trust 1989-94. Before joining Avonmore Foods plc he was chief accountant of Downes Buttercrust Bakery, and secretary and director of administration at Bord Bainne – the Irish Dairy Board. He is a member of the Institute of Cost and Management Accountants.

Roy Bailie is chairman of W & G Baird Holdings Ltd, a British and Irish packaging, printing and publishing group. In 1977 he led the management buy-out of W & G Baird Ltd from the British Printing Confederation. He has been an active member of the BPIF – British Printing Industries Federation, and was chairman of the North West Region for over two years, the only

Northern Irishman to hold this post. In addition, he has served on the Wages Negotiation Committee of the BPIF and is also a member of the executive board of management of the Federation. Directorships include Biddles Ltd, Guildford; Biddles (Bookbinders) Ltd, Kings Lynn; Textflow Services Ltd, and Blackstaff Press Ltd. In addition, he is a director of the IDB – the Industrial Development Board, Tacade – the Advisory Council on Alcohol & Drug Education, the Northern Ireland Tourist Board and the Bank of Ireland (Northern Ireland Advisory Board).

Finbar Callanan has been director general of The Institution of Engineers of Ireland since 1979, having been president from 1974 to 1975. He is a member of the Register Commission of FEANI, the European engineering qualifications body, and was president of their Industrial Commission for a number of years. In 1991 he was conferred MA MAI (Honoris Causa) by Trinity College Dublin in the Sesquicentenary of the School of Engineering. In 1996 he received an LLD (Honoris Causa) from the NCEA – National Council for Educational Awards, for his contribution to Irish engineering and to the NCEA.
Finbar Callanan has also worked with the Office of Public Works, the harbour commissioners and consultants, and Bord na Móna.

Eileen O'Mara Walsh is founding chairperson of Forbairt, the state agency established in 1994 to promote the development of Irish indigenous industry. She is also managing director of O'Mara Travel Company Ltd and has worked in the tourism and travel industry in Ireland for over twenty years. In addition, she is chairperson of Heritage Island Ltd which was established in 1992 to promote Ireland's major heritage attractions. From 1984 to 1991 Eileen O'Mara Walsh was chairperson of Great Southern Hotels and continues to serve on the board. A former director of Aer Lingus, she was founding chairman of the Irish Tourist Industry Confederation. She also served on the government-appointed Task Force on Tourism in 1992 and was appointed to the National Tourism Council in 1994.

Padraic A White was managing director of IDA Ireland – the Industrial Development Authority of Ireland – from 1981 to 1990. Under his leadership the IDA developed an international reputation for Ireland as a country noted for its young educated population – the Young European concept – and attracted international companies in the knowledge- and technology-intensive industries.

Since 1990 Padraic White has moved into the private sector and is director of a number of Irish and international companies, including Dresdner Bank group's companies in Ireland, London Life Re-Insurance, the Custom House Dock Development Authority, the Industrial Credit Corporation. He is chairman of the BRW Insurance and Financial Services group and of the Northside Partnership Ltd. In addition, he is a member of the executive committee of the Economic and Social Research Institute and of the board of trustees of the Eisenhower Exchange Fellowships Inc.

David Kennedy is former chief executive of Aer Lingus (1974-88) and former chairman of the Irish National Petroleum Corporation (1979-92). He was deputy governor of the Bank of Ireland, and chairman of the Irish Management Institute and of Co-operation North. He is currently chairman of Drury Communications Ltd, and Drury Sports Management Ltd, and holds a number of non-executive directorships, including CRH plc, Lifetime Insurance, Jury's Hotel Group plc and Global Aircraft Leasing Ltd.

Since 1989 he has been part-time professor of strategic marketing in University College Dublin, and has also worked as a management consultant for a number of international companies and for several Irish government departments.

Dr Edward Walsh is president of the University of Limerick, and was chairman of its planning board from 1970 to 1975. Under his direction the University has become renowned as one of Ireland's most forward-thinking and technologically-advanced third-level centres. He is also founding chairman of the National Technological Park, Ireland's first science park, as well as founding chairman of both the National Council for Curriculum and Assessment and the National Self-Portrait Collection of Ireland. He has also served as a member and chairman of the board of the Shannon Development Company.

Dr Walsh is a Fellow of the Royal Society of the Arts and a member of the Royal Hibernian Academy of Arts. He is a vice president of the International Association of University Presidents and a member of the New York Academy of Science.

Foreword

The RDS was founded in 1731 to promote the development of agriculture, industry, science, and the useful arts. With the year 2000 approaching, the RDS Committee of Industry decided to invite twenty-one leading Irish business people to sketch out their visions of business and industry in Ireland twenty-five years hence and I was designated to coordinate and edit the contributions.

The authors were encouraged to take risks, and to prophesy from the perspective of their individual business experiences. The views expressed are not necessarily shared by the editor or the RDS. The contributors were selected from specific sectors such as agribusiness, arts and culture, banking, computers, construction, education, electrical machinery, employer and employee representation, industrial development, insurance, natural resources, retailing and telecommunications. The result, which the reader can judge for himself or herself, is intended to weave a rich and varied tapestry depicting the scene in the year 2020.

The path of progress can be obscured by short-term and often random events. Many of the contributors to this publication have chosen to describe both the ultimate destination, and the intermediate steps in precise terms. Others have adopted a more abstract approach. The following are some personal reflections.

The island is currently in the process of re-establishing its international economic position. In the mid-eighteenth century, prior to the industrial revolution, Ireland's population was greater than that of other small European countries such as the Netherlands, Sweden or Switzerland; and greater than that of the combined populations of Finland, Norway and Denmark. This situation persisted until the middle of the nineteenth century.

However, Ireland's lack of participation in the industrial revolution and resultant over-reliance on agriculture, left the country ill-prepared to cope with the impact of the Great Famine of 1945-47 or to maintain its population even at the post-Famine level. For over a century the population of the island was set on a downward spiral.

Then in the late 1950s the population collapse was arrested as the economy of the South, then an independent Republic, started to expand vigorously. New industries and technologies were attracted from abroad. The economy was modernised, protectionism was dismantled, and over the next thirty years the population increased by 25%, a faster rate of increase than that of most European countries. Nevertheless, the population of the island is still considerably below the scale achieved compared to other small European economies in the eighteenth century. I pose the question as to which is the best indicator of the long-term trend – the high relative population of the late eighteenth and early nineteenth centuries, or the low relative population of the first half of the twentieth century?

The population of Ireland has always been influenced not only by the natural increase – the difference between births and deaths – but also by net migration. During recent decades emigration has slowed down dramatically. In the 1970s emigration became, temporarily, immigration. The current accelerating rate of increase in employment seems likely to result in a recurrence of immigration so that an island population of six million is achievable within the time limit of this book's vision.

Since 1990 there has been a marked change in the dependency ratio, that is the number of people in the economy compared to those in paid employment. This has significant implications for Irish per capita incomes and therefore for living standards. While the incomes of those at work in recent decades have been close to the average in the European Union, incomes per capita were always much lower because of our persistently high dependency ratio, bloated by large numbers of women working at home, large numbers of young children, and high employment. The dependency ratio is now falling sharply and on current trends will be in line with the average in the European Union at the start of the new millennium. This implies that Irish incomes per capita will also be at or near average European levels. Having closed a gap of about one-third over the last quarter of this century, is the process likely to stop there? It is not impossible that, stimulated by the more rapid adoption of new technological advances than most other western European countries, Irish incomes may begin to move significantly ahead of average European levels.

Three of the most noteworthy developments of the late twentieth century are particularly favourable to the Irish economy. I refer to air transport, information technology, and the freeing of international trade. Together these developments mean that concepts such as peripherality and an island economy are more a state of mind than an accurate reflection of reality.

Air transport has become safer, faster and less costly, and fortunately aeroplanes do not differentiate between land and water so that islands become irrelevant. Travel by air in Europe now exceeds travel by train. The Dublin-London air corridor is the second busiest in Europe after London-Paris. More than twice the population now travels on or off the island annually by air or sea. If current rates of growth are sustained, passenger flows in 2020 will be eight times greater than the resident population. This will lead not only to a burgeoning tourism industry but also to a quadrupling of the number of Irish executives commuting to work in cities within an hour's travel arc from their nearest regional airport.

Information technology is a second important influence. This is an era when messages are sent around the globe in the form of voice, data, or images in microseconds. The same service can be supplied at a distance of 10m or 10,000km. Countries that have, like Ireland, an advanced telecommunications network are at the 'centre of the world'. Higher value-added products such as financial data, publications, computer programmes, or films can be transmitted or received instantaneously through a worldwide network. Many of these products are produced by individuals or small groups of professionals engaged in teleworking. It is feasible that within twenty-five years there will be more people employed in trading these products internationally than in the whole of manufacturing industry.

A third major influence on Ireland now and in the future is the commitment to a fully open trading economy. The great majority of Irish-made products and internationally-traded services is exported. Therefore, the gains from having free access to export markets far outweigh the benefits which would arise from protecting the home market. Protectionism has been dismantled, and international economic disciplines have been adopted. These changes have brought about a substantial attitudinal change in Irish industrialists. There are few cities in Europe where they are not to be found trading or seeking out innovative ideas. The vitality of a young well-educated labour force, and the confidence created by a track record of trading successfully abroad have generated a dynamism in Irish business which has probably never been experienced before.

Finally, the establishment at the end of 1992 of a Single

European Market permitting the free movement of goods, capital, people and the freedom to provide services has resulted in a single market on this island also for the first time in over almost three quarters of a century. Physical, psychological, fiscal, and security barriers had reduced the level of trade between the two parts of the island to about one-third of what might have been expected in a 'normal' open market. The removal of customs posts at the border, and the return of peace throughout the island in September 1994 have already had a substantial positive impact on economic development in Northern Ireland and the Republic.

Greater intra island trade will replace imports. It will also increase the quantity and quality of local suppliers so vital to the location of large firms in Ireland. It has been estimated that up to 75,000 additional jobs will be generated when the single market on the island reaches its potential. Only the psychological barriers now remain. These will have disappeared long before 2020.

The original members of the RDS in the eighteenth century were required, as a condition of membership, to investigate a branch of industry in Ireland, to compare its performance with that in other countries and to make recommendations to their peers on the action to be taken for its improvement. The essays in this book represent the views of experienced Irish business people on the nature of the changes which they foresee in many sectors of industry over the next twenty-five years, and are presented to the reader for discussion and debate. It is hoped that they will also stimulate action to overcome perceived obstacles to development, and to contribute to the peace, prosperity, and progress not only of the Irish people but also of the wider international community. I wish to thank the authors for their willingness to share with us their views of the future. I am satisfied that together, in the imagery of WB Yeats, they have looked up in the 'sun's eye', and have indeed given us 'the right twigs for an eagle's nest'.

I also wish to thank Frances Power of the O'Brien Press for her assistance in editing, my colleagues on the RDS Committee of Industry for their trust and encouragement, and particularly Carol Tyndall for her good-humoured persistence in obtaining the scripts on time.

Liam Connellan
Vice President, RDS
December 1995

JAMES P CULLITON

RDS Industry Gold Medal Lecture 2020 [1]

James P Culliton is chairman of the Allied Irish Banks plc group, Unidare plc, and Northern Telecom (Ireland) Ltd.

I am very pleased and honoured to accept the RDS Industry Gold Medal. This Society was established nearly three hundred years ago 'for the advancement of agriculture, other branches of industry, science and art'. While the relative importance of agriculture has declined, the spirit underlying the Society's objective of promoting advancement and innovation in different fields of activity is of even greater relevance today than in the eighteenth century and the Society has an unrivalled tradition of achievement in these areas.

The third recipient of the RDS Gold Medal was also Chairman of AIB during a critical period in the development of that organisation, which has greatly prospered in the intervening twenty-six years. During the course of his lecture he set out some themes which I think are of continued relevance today and to which I will return later. But first, let me review where we are.

IRELAND'S SUCCESS

Last year we were delighted to see that Ireland had the highest NW (national welfare) per head in the world. As you know, ten years ago we abandoned GNP as a measure of our economic and social progress and substituted NW as a much better measure of the quality of life, as it included important elements such as environmental quality, level of crime and accidents. This, of course, made much more sense. We all recognise now that a road accident prevented contributes much more to the quality of life than fifty broken legs cared for.

Our great success has shown how wise the policy changes we made in the 1990s were, despite the virulent criticisms made of them at the time. A critical factor in this success was the adoption by government of the Vision 2010 Strategy proposed by the then Minister Ruairi Quinn – whom we are delighted to see here this evening.

This Vision, which many thought was pie in the sky, turned out to be much less than we achieved, much like the aims set out in the Lemass/Whitaker programme in the 1950s.

Let me remind you of the Vision 2010 objectives:
  ▶ achieve the average per capita income of the European Union;
  ▶ provide full employment for those seeking work;
  ▶ have the best preserved and the best managed environment in the European Union;
  ▶ possess the most efficient and effective public administration in Europe;
  ▶ be perceived, outside Europe, as the best place to invest, and do business within Europe.

Crucial to the achievement of Vision 2010 was the ten-year programme of budgetary measures, aimed at rewarding work, promoting enterprise and increasing social solidarity, which was launched in 1995. Due to the constraints, it often appeared that progress was agonisingly slow, yet the cumulative effect of the measures went a considerable distance within a few short years towards improving the climate for innovation, risk taking and wealth creation while maintaining social cohesion by ensuring that the weaker elements in society were protected.

Europe has been crucial to our success. We are now a

respected member of the top tier of the European Union which currently has thirty members. We should recognise the courage of our leaders in taking the decision in the year 2002 to adopt the European Single Currency despite the decision by Britain to stay out. This has not been an easy road, but the response to the challenges posed by our strategic decision to join the EU First Division has paid off handsomely.

The assessment twenty-five years ago that Ireland's contribution to the European Union was unspectacular makes very strange reading today. This assessment, of the first twenty years of our membership, was that Ireland 'makes little original contribution to strategic policy formulation, whether from modesty, reticence or neglect, but more likely from a supposedly realistic appraisal of its standing. Such realism is the enemy of the idealism offered by the founding fathers from the smaller Member States, and it is certainly a pity if it deters a potential flow of good ideas from Ireland ...'[2] A statement such as this would be inconceivable now.

INSTITUTIONAL CHANGE

The boost to our economy arising from the resolution of the political problems of our island in 1999 was a major contributory factor to our growth. This also gave rise to a significant review of our political institutions which had not been working well – this was clear from the fact that in the thirty years since 1969 no government had succeeded in being re-elected.

The new Constitution of Ireland's Second Republic was adopted in 1999 and made major changes to the system of government. This provided for a classic separation of powers under a directly elected chief executive who reported to a smaller Dáil of a hundred members and a Senate of thirty members. Under the new arrangements ministers could not be members of either House of the Oireachtas and it was possible to recruit people of proven talent and expertise from business, trade unions and academic life to serve in government. Prior to that the demands of our electoral system of proportional representation meant that people of proven expertise found it very difficult to enter politics in mid-career. Charges of elitism were rebuffed by the fact that the Executive was made clearly accountable to the Oireachtas, a point symbolised by the fact that the Ceann Comhairle is also now Head of State. The amalgamation of the offices of President and Ceann Comhairle was mooted after the highly successful term of office of President Mary Robinson led to considerable difficulties in finding a candidate able to succeed her.

This institutional change also led to the most significant re-organisation of the civil service since the Northcote-Trevelyan reform of the nineteenth century. This re-organisation had its genesis in a number of reforms in the previous two decades, notably the establishment of the Top Level Appointments Committee in 1984, the Strategic Management Initiative which began in 1994, the introduction of Freedom of Information legislation in 1996 and the amendments to the Ministers and Secretaries Act of 1924 which abolished the outdated concept of the corporation *sole* in 1997 and made secretaries of government departments (who were retitled directors general) accountable for the efficient and effective management of their departments.[3] The new directors general were able to streamline civil service administration to a degree which surprised even the optimists and provided us with a central administration which is the envy of other countries for the quality of its service.

An important additional factor was the revitalisation of local government in Ireland following the adoption of the principle of subsidiarity in the Constitution. This meant that minor local matters which had previously cluttered central departments were dealt with at local level.

We now have the most advanced public sector and tax system

in the world. It was particularly gratifying to note that last year the national debt was finally repaid and the National Treasury Management Agency disbanded. This was the latest among a number of state agencies who achieved the ultimate success of completing their work. The trend was set by the board of the Industrial Development Authority (IDA) some years ago, when it approached the government to say that its brief had been fulfilled and that it was no longer necessary to have an industrial development agency.

The policy of reducing the growth in public expenditure below the rate of growth in the economy, which has been followed consistently over the last twenty-five years, has paid remarkable dividends. The payroll tax which was an economic anachronism was finally removed in 2009 (the centenary of Lloyd George's famous budget which introduced old-age pensions) and we are well on our way towards abolishing income tax. These achievements were helped by the discovery of substantial oil reserves in the Porcupine Basin in the early years of this century but were due mainly to the consistent economic and social policy followed since before the turn of the century.

THE INNOVATION SOCIETY

How did we achieve all this? My predecessor noted in his 1994 lecture that 'Innovation is the central issue in economic prosperity'. The short answer is that we took this seriously.

How did we create a culture of innovation? We substantially increased investment in research and development. Expenditure on research and development in Ireland is now the highest in Europe, but still lags behind China. A survey of international industrialists placed Ireland in the top ten of fifty OECD countries in its capacity for innovation.

The state became much more involved in promoting the application of new technology. This was necessary because without state support, investment in technology would be too low because of risk and high costs and because many of the benefits that arise from successful technology investment are external to the firm.

A very important contributory factor to our success was the sustained investment in education over the last half-century. In addition to the intrinsic merits of education, the quality of our people as a result of this investment has made Ireland very attractive as a location in which to do business.

We also changed the attitude of Irish people to change. The reality of the need to be competitive finally dawned in the latter years of the last century and the result was a massive change in public attitudes. People realised that the only way to stay competitive was to change faster than the competition. Trade union attitudes were crucial. We were fortunate to have gifted leadership of our trade union movement which actively promoted change as the best means of increasing prosperity.

The results of our policies may be seen clearly in the success of our large pure food industry which is now exporting to five continents. Our application of developments in genetic engineering has transformed this business in the last two decades. I would like to acknowledge the role of the Royal Dublin Society in identifying and promoting the potential in this area at a very early stage. This has been an important factor in our success.

FINANCIAL SERVICES

Before concluding, let me say a few words about some of the exciting developments in the financial services industry. The advances in technology have transformed the money system

- debit cards and Smart Cards together with the supporting EFTPOS (Electronic Funds Transfer at Point of Sale) infrastructure have displaced cheques, notes and coin as the form of payment for medium to small value transactions.

> much personal contact with the bank is now carried out from the home using interactive video to the bank manager via secure Cable TV or powerful PCs, which are now in 90% of all homes. The bank manager is available at a time and a place that suits the customer.

Technology way back in the nineties was just beginning to impact on everyday lives. Your thermostat kept the temperature in your house the way you liked it, your video recorder taped your favourite TV programmes when you were out, your answering machine took telephone calls for you. Now in 2020, software agents do the same sort of thing in computer networks – work for you while you do something else.

They sort electronic mail (scrapping the junk!!), select articles for personalised newspapers and even go shopping for you in the virtual marketplace.

For financial services:

> the information superhighway is now the prime channel used by customers searching for best value in the purchase of goods extending right across the EU! This is enabled by these software programs which are known as intelligent agents or 'knowbots' operating from the home PC. On receipt of goods, payment is made directly from your bank account – using the Smart Card for unique authorisation.

For business, most financial controllers now frequently use their individual data scouts, (a version of the software agent-driven programs that browse information). These scouts, housed on the individual's PC, access the Internet, explore developments of specific interest to the business and make decisions on what to report back to executives at regular intervals throughout the day (see PC Week, January 9, 1995).

This has had massive implications for the networks of banks and building societies. It is interesting to visit banking museums and look at safes and strongrooms which are completely redundant today.

29

The transformation of the banking industry in the early years of this century made life very difficult for those who had grown up in a non-competitive culture. This resulted in a major shake-out of the industry and led to the establishment of the three major Irish financial institutions we see today.

The main task of large companies and the biggest contribution they can make to the community is to do the job they have to do as well as possible. In this way they discharge their major community responsibility. It is not to create jobs, sponsor festivals or be a charitable institution. If they do their main job well, this will make the maximum contribution to the growth of wealth and employment in Ireland. Anything else is incidental. By focusing on our major responsibility to provide effective and efficient financial services, I believe that we have made a significant contribution to Irish success over the last twenty-five years.

CONCLUSION

While Ireland has made progress on a scale that would have been regarded as very optimistic by those living twenty-five years ago, we must not be complacent. We still face significant challenges; not least that posed by our aging demographic structure which our partner countries have faced before us. Unfortunately we did not begin to address this issue in good time and the scale of the adjustment that we face over the next few years poses substantial challenges.

However, let us face the future with the confidence shown in much more difficult circumstances by previous generations.

We are a small country and as the Red Queen said to Alice in Wonderland: 'In this place you have to run very fast just to stand still.'

We have been running very fast. Our problems have been clearly identified. Now we must act decisively to address the challenges that face us in the future.

FOOTNOTES

1. This chapter is written in the form of a lecture delivered in the year 2020.

2. 'Ireland's Contribution to the European Union', Dermot Scott, Institute of European Affairs, Occasional Paper 4, 1994, p38.

3. 'Under the Ministers and Secretaries Act, 1924, each minister is a corporation *sole* and as such in law must make all decisions relating to their department', (Devlin Report, Appendix 1, paragraph 3.2). In law the minister and the department have no separate powers; the minister is the department. This provides the legal basis for the phrase in letters from government departments: 'I am directed by the Minister ...'

Eddie O'Connor

Interview from STUDIES, 2021

Eddie O'Connor is managing director of Bord na Móna, and a member of the boards of the Irish Management Institute and the Institute of Directors.

What follows is an interview by Veronica McPartland with Professor Rainus McAuley taken from the July issue of STUDIES in the year 2021.

In the introduction to the interview Veronica McPartland said: 'On a world stage there are few who would challenge Professor McAuley's right to speak authoritatively on recent social, economic and political developments. Having qualified ex. UCD in the early nineties of the last century he worked with three multinationals over the next fifteen years. During this time he made several break-throughs in the fields of genetic engineering and cancer research. This phase of his life coincided with his discovery of the key role played by the human liver in regulating the formation of cancer in the human body. He found that a naturally-produced enzyme lipochrome G470 could catalyse natural cell reproduction into cancer-forming uncontrolled reproduction. This was to be his last endeavour in pure research.

'His work with lipochrome G470 led to the formation of a new implant procedure which took years to get clearance through the increasingly regulated political compliance structure. He found it very difficult to reconcile the death toll from the thirty-three types of cancer that could be controlled by the new procedure with the slowness of bureaucracy. The impatience which had always been evident in his research work now grew and seemed to propel him into a headlong confrontation with several national bureaucracies. What had appeared to be an isolated problem – bureaucracy dealing with a life-enhancing new procedure – on investigation turned out to be democracy's great problem in dealing with innovation.

'Professor McAuley began to work, as a consultant at first, on the practical ways of dealing with technological break-throughs at regulatory level.

'After much research a series of proposals emerged. These were of such importance that a Directorate of the EU was created under the Professor's leadership. Its job was to implement his ground-breaking proposals on democracy and regulation.

'Professor McAuley now chairs a world grouping to oversee the possibilities of short-circuiting the processes of democratising Africa and South America.'

So, Professor, you have seen many changes over the past twenty-five years. Could you say which were the most important?

You could divide the changes into three broad categories, technological, political and social. All are interconnected but it is probably fair to say that technology is the main driver for change. It is the *primus inter pares*.

What were the most important technological changes?

I have noticed that the greatest break-through came where two or more technologies emerging from different scientific and engineering disciplines came together. With this in mind I think one of the most significant developments was the HIOs (Head-up Intelligent Optics) or Smart Glasses that came along in 2001. The human race looked as if it was going to be swamped with data before that date. The 986 chip, which effectively led to the micro-miniaturisation of the computer, brought the first true user-friendly capability. This user friendship became apparent when the computation and data storage aspects of computers was allied to voice activation, broadcasting and head-up display (HUD).

I remember the wonder of wearing my first pair of HIOs. They functioned as a perfectly ordinary pair of sight correctors in traditional glasses mode. When, however, I asked the price of Heinz shares, I was delighted to read the price as of twelve noon that day displayed on the upper portion of my glasses. HUD technology combined optics with holography. The device was powered by a 986 processor and a tiny battery and looked like the hearing aid of former generations. People were able to wear this discrete device attached to the part of their glasses that sat around the ear.

This invention put the human in interactive communication with the extended Internet. It might have been thought that its greatest impact would be in business, whereas in fact it was really as an educational aid that its impact was most felt. Children were able to call up maps, could interact with some educational cartoons and could learn while they played. Somehow it seemed that the imagination and the feeling part of the brain was freer to develop once the burden of memorising a vast array of facts was removed.

A second technological change was the development of the hypersonic commercial transport. The plane which was jointly developed by Boeing and Airbus carried five hundred people up into near outer space and was able to do the Los Angeles to Tokyo run in three hours, Frankfurt to Sydney in four hours. What made this invention so interesting was the introduction and use of the Ion Plasma (IP) drive.

The IP engine was itself a ground-breaking example of risk reduction in business. Five of the world's biggest companies collaborated on the research that led to the IP prototype and first working engine. The development costs amounted to $20 billion and were spent over a ten-year period. Three different governments (Germany, the US and Japan) had to coordinate their R&D subventions. The project came near to breaking down on several occasions when governments changed or the profitability of one of the five participating companies took a short-term setback.

One of the interesting side effects of this great coordinated research effort was the reconstruction of the ozone layer that the emissions from the IP drive allowed. It would be true to say that no one really knew anything much about the ozone layer before the IP consortium proposed to break through it several times every hour. Some $2 billion of the total research spend was associated with describing and coming to an understanding of the chemistry of the ozone layer.

The world became a global village from the information viewpoint from the 1970s on; it became a physical village from the year 2010.

Have you observed any change in human nature during your lifetime, perhaps resulting from the incredible advances in technology?

It is interesting that you ask that question now. As far as I would be concerned the answer is a fairly emphatic No. I would have to admit that it is difficult to prove one way or the other.

We know the average height of the species has increased by four inches since the 1950s. We know that three-quarters of the world's population are literate, numerate and technologically aware now. What we don't know is whether the cranium size has increased or what has happened to the average weight of the brain.

My thesis is based on the fact that the environment of the world, or more importantly of the ecosphere, has remained constant. Critically the amount of oxygen, nitrogen and all the other gases are unchanged since the human species first emerged. *Homo sapiens,* so long as it lives on the surface of this planet, does not need to change or evolve to survive. When one reads the thoughts of the ancient Greeks, and in particular Plutarch, on the subject of politics and social organisation, you realise they are describing people as we see them around us now. Again in the Middle Ages the essay by Francis Bacon on 'Simulation and Dissimulation', the works of Shakespeare and Machiavelli are so perfect in their understanding of our current human nature that I must conclude that at core we remain the same.

The words of Hegel, however, run around inside my head. He pointed out that change happens quantitatively, little bit upon little but for a long period of time. Suddenly something happens to make one look at the before and after situation and one realises that a qualitative change has occurred; that maybe the relationships of humans, one with the other, have altered in a deep way. Maybe something is happening to us slowly and subtly.

However I think not.

Space travel will adjust our genetic make-up. When we humans land on some earth-like planet in another solar system and are forced to evolve or to die out, then I believe human nature will change. A new near-human species will emerge from our current gene pool.

Your own work, Professor, on cancer research was pretty groundbreaking. How would you stack up its importance alongside other changes in medical science over the past twenty-five years?

By far the most important work was that which led to the understanding of the human immune system. Up to the year 2000 disease had been dealt with largely by antibiotics. It would be more appropriate to say that antibiotics interfered with the reproduction of microbes and the real work was done by that masterpiece of evolution, the human immune system. By the late 1990s several significant simultaneous occurrences were causing research to be focused with increasing intensity on the immune system. Hospitals had become dangerous places. The only microbes which lived there were those which had survived by mutation, the attacks of all known antibiotics. People went in for harmless operations and contracted almost incurable diseases; some even died. The HIV virus was pandemic.

In a major onslaught, lasting ten years in thirty-one different countries and with the backing of every drug company, the truth about the immune system was unravelled. The sciences of microbiology, immunology, serology, genetics, information technology, x-ray optics and holography and many others were interfaced to build a paradigm of the genetic basis of the immune systems. Countless blind alleys were entered. Measurement equipment was developed where the speed of an individual electron influenced the outcome of the observation.

Science and technology were changed forever during the course of this struggle. Alongside the classical scientific method with its always increasing specialisation, the interfacing sciences began to emerge. More and more it became apparent that important and commercial truths lay at the boundaries of different branches of science.

Not only did we cure AIDS, but we also became empowered to interfere with the genetic code to do away with Down's Syndrome, cystic fibrosis and a host of other genetic disorders.

It is difficult listening to you, Professor, to reconcile these great break-throughs with the still real existence of wars and poverty. Why have people not progressed as far with the social sciences and political economy as we have in the areas you have been describing?

The answer lies in the reality of human nature itself. People still want power. Power always corrupts. People are still angry, envious and greedy. Those parts of our nature are very deep within us.

Human hope is a powerful driving force for good, but if dashed it can become a vengeful force for destruction. The ancients tried to describe human nature in terms of good and evil. Indeed it was the realisation that every human had the tendency to be both good and evil that led to the ethical basis of all religions.

Just a minute, Professor, you mention religion. Would you like to give an overview on what has happened to the official religions over the past while?

Throughout history religion has played a number of key human and social functions. Each transition to a new social order seemed to have been accompanied by the emergence of a new code of behaviour. This code was lived by the founding fathers. It was, in all the major religions, studied by intelligent ones and written down. This partially dealt with the problem of transmitting the new religion from generation to generation. The study of human culture will show how written words contain the rules, but spoken or oral tradition plays a reinforcing role. Myths and legends which are passed on to children, almost before they can walk and talk, are probably more important than the written ethical code.

The core however is the ethical code. The Ten Commandments was the Jewish core, the Sermon on the Mount was the Christian extension of Jewish beliefs. In essence, these ethical codes were guiding beacons for the civilisation of the day. The Protestant ethic of the German-Swiss capitalists was the code needed to move humankind from the stagnation of the Middle Ages to the self-help, wealth-creation outlook of the new era. To make sure that they were obeyed, classical religions interposed the idea of an overwhelming outside force which would hand out reward or punishment according to whether one obeyed the code. God was and possibly is a very necessary human invention.

The need for an ethical basis to society is precisely as relevant today as it was in AD 1020 or 2000 BC.

Religions are human creations, supported in one way or

another by an institutional bulwark. Human institutions atrophy and are in need of constant and sustained renewal.

There was a refusal by the Catholic Church to recognise the role of women or to recognise the need for priests to marry right up to the end of the last century. You know that the church once had 'liberated' women, at least by comparison to their treatment by other religions. It was a symbol of official atrophy that it should have become attached to a much lesser and dependent role for women until quite recently.

The need to establish an ethical basis for the new business, work, global village and informational environments was one of the great problems faced by mankind around the year 2000.

It began to be studied seriously by business, the universities and by governments around this time and indeed still is.

However, it is most gratifying to see the official religions coming in from the cold and taking on board the new realities. Recognising that it is as sinful to read private information about someone else as it is to steal from them has been a great step forward. Liberation theology has been reinterpreted to mean the setting free of the ordinary person from the potential tyranny of information prisonerhood.

What was the change over the past twenty-five years which has given you the most pleasure?

Even though I have been working at EU and world level for the past fifteen years, I still get most pleasure from viewing what happened in Ireland during that time.

Post-colonialism finished up, a washed-out force, in the 1990s. The new generation of Irish people began at last to innovate their way out of the vicious circle of unemployment and low growth.

Some of the change began in the schools. A cadre of teachers began to see that technology and business actually could create wealth and free their students from having to emigrate. They stopped preaching about a mythical 'environment' (which never existed) and started teaching that the environment is a human creation and a source of massive opportunity.

The work done by Forbairt was crucial to the creation of the entrepreneurial society. It lost no opportunity to promote and celebrate native brilliance. The way it led new strategic thinking in the food industry and wind energy industries were object lessons in industrial development.

Coordination between universities and industry happened quicker and with greater effect in Ireland. Competitive advantage comes to those who can generate, protect and commercialise new knowledge. Several good examples of this use of universities emerged in Ireland. The 'Island of Saints and Scholars' wasn't such a bad place to be born. This was particularly so when one saw an old tradition and culture being reinterpreted to give the nation competitive advantage.

One of the bulwarks of the post-colonial establishment was the state bureaucracy. It was generalist, non-economic and non-technological in its approach.

Late twentieth-century Irish bureaucracy had much in common with the British Civil Service of the nineteenth century. Technology was a given. People who were qualified as technologists were thought to be unfit to run a government department. As a result the spend on R&D was small. As technological risks are very hard to assess without training in its basics, the bureaucracy's response was to be risk averse.

From my point of view bureaucracy's inability to manage risk was its biggest failing. Ireland had pottered along at a discounted rate of growth of 4% (discounting the subvention from Europe and the multinational black hole).

By 1999 Ireland was declassified as an EU Objective 1 country. To get EU funding into any part of Ireland, the country had to be divided into regions. Some of these regions met the criteria for funding. Of itself this change reversed the centralisation drive of the 1960s and 1970s. New democratic structures were built up.

The sense of ownership and belonging which had characterised many European countries came belatedly to the remoter regions in Ireland. It was great to see the replacement of the political clientelism that had characterised much of rural life with a new spirit of self help. The people, (indeed, any people, anywhere) are well able to manage themselves in regional blocks that make sense if they are trusted and empowered to do it.

From about 2002 onwards the genius of the Irish, kept well hidden since 1920, blossomed. It was the most enjoyable change I saw in my lifetime.

Senator Feargal Quinn

The Customer's Kingdom

Senator Feargal Quinn is managing director of the Superquinn group and the author of *Crowning the Customer*.

In one important sense my vision of the retailing and distribution
scene in Ireland in 2020 is very clear, very precise. In another less
important sense, the vision is vague and undefined.

I am vague about what exactly the distribution scene will look
like:

- will we have gigantic shopping centres that people will
  travel fifty or sixty miles to visit?
- will we have revitalised, vibrant high streets, bringing back
  to Ireland some of the traditional hustle and bustle of the
  thriving market town?
- will we have shops at all, as we know them now – or will
  they have gone the way of the horse and buggy, yielding
  to a form of buying and selling that is completely technology-based?
- will cash have totally disappeared as a medium of exchange, to be replaced by electronic alternatives?

Of course, it's fun to speculate about such things, but I am not so
sure that it is very much more than that. In particular, I am not
sure that it is wise to base decisions for investment or the planning
of national infrastructure on the basis of what it might technologically be possible to do. Between the technological *possibility* and
the market *reality* there can be a vast gap, a gap into which unlimited
amounts of resources can be thrown with no return at all.

However, I believe that sensible planning and investment decisions can be based on two aspects of my vision for 2020 that are very precise:

> that in 2020 Irish customers, for whatever product or service, will be able to buy *what* they want, *when* they want, *where* they want, and *how* they want;

> that in 2020 Europe will have become a single market-place very similar to what now exists in the United States.

I foresee an Irish market-place that will be totally customer-driven, and the physical shape of the market-place will reflect that fact above all.

I believe that by 2020, and perhaps well before, the trend towards the customer's kingdom will have reached its conclusion. And if we want to imagine the difference between then and now, we have only to ask ourselves in what ways customers in Ireland do not currently enjoy these capabilities.

Take, for instance, the capability of buying what you want. Since the beginning of the industrial revolution at least, this capability has been greatly restricted. Modern manufacturing, until very recently, has been based firmly on the principle of the mass market and the long production run. Though increasingly based on market demand in a very general sense, the industrial approach has always tended to force the customer into a strait-jacket. Sure, you had choice – but it was a very limited choice, and one dictated in the last analysis by what suited the manufac-turer.

We have moved a long way from the days when Henry Ford could say: 'They can have any colour they like so long as it's black.' But we have not moved all the way along the road, by any means. And this is something that will change the face of retailing and much else besides.

The trend we are talking about here is a powerful shift. In recent years it's been customary to think about this as a shift in power from the manufacturer of the product to the distributor of it. We have seen the growth of retailing chains, we have seen in many countries the massive development of retailers' own brands. Originally conceived of as just a cheap alternative to manufacturers' brands, these are now emerging as fully-fledged products in their own right – particularly in the area of value-added foods.

I think, however, that to see this power shift as merely from the manufacturer to the distributor is to misunderstand fundamentally what is going on. Looked at from the perspective of 2020, I believe that the long-term trend is a shift in power from the person who makes the product to the person who ultimately buys and uses it. The retailer is, in truth, just a proxy for the end-customer. At the end of the day the power will rest with the individual customer.

What does this mean in practice? It means that in 2020 the customer will be able to demand from the manufacturing/distributing complex products and services that correspond much more closely to their individual needs and tastes.

We have all experienced the frustration of asking for a particular thing in a retail situation, and being told, 'There's no demand for that, sorry.' As a customer, we're sometimes tempted to respond, 'But *I'm* demanding it.' Most of the time, though, we tend to accept that if our needs are out of step with the pattern of mass demand, we have to go without.

That is changing fast, and will have changed utterly by 2020. This is not to say that the mass market will disappear. On the contrary: some mass markets will grow bigger, and this has implications for the concentration of manufacturing units to achieve economies of scale. But side by side with that, we will see the fragmentation of some mass markets into a multiplicity of tiny markets in which the emphasis is on meeting the individual customer's specific needs as closely as possible.

Already we can envisage a situation in which cars will be custom-built. You will choose from a long menu of possibilities, tailoring your choice exactly to your needs. These requirements will be transmitted (instantly and automatically) to the manufacturing unit, who will put together what will in practice be almost an individual car.

This is far from being a totally new idea; what *is* new is the extent to which we are going to see it generalised. If we look for a moment twenty-five years back instead of forward, we see an Ireland in which pizzas had never been heard of. Nowadays, of course, pizzas are a very significant part of the food economy.

But what I want to highlight is that when pizzas first came into the retail world the approach was to treat them as an industrial product – mass produced, with a very limited range of options. What we noticed as retailers was that people's taste in pizzas was anything but homogeneous. You like pepperoni, I hate it. The ideal would be to make individual pizzas to reflect these preferences.

At the time that was anathema in retailing terms. You could do that at home, if you were making your own pizzas. You could do it in a restaurant that cooked each order on the spot. But in a shop ...

I'm talking history here, of course, because now you can buy an individual pizza in a shop. To make that possible we had as retailers to get into the manufacturing business – not in some remote factory, but on the shop floor in front of the customers' eyes. To supply this emerging need, we became manufacturers. Perhaps it would be truer to say that we became restaurateurs. However you describe it, this little story is a case history in adapting to the emerging trend of giving the customer what they actually want, as opposed to giving them what it suits us (or a manufacturer) to provide.

This is, however, only one area in which the customer is beginning to take control. Shopping is about a lot more than buying what you want.

When you buy what you buy is an important issue to shoppers, especially as people's lives become more complex and as shopping becomes more a family activity than one carried out just by a house-bound spouse.

It's fascinating to look around the world at the different practices. Already, in the US, time is not an issue: you can shop when it suits you, not when it suits the shop. Increasingly there, supermarkets are open twenty-four hours a day, seven days a week. They are rapidly becoming, in fact, convenience stores.

On the other hand, some countries within the EU are far more restricted in shopping hours than we are here in Ireland. It comes as quite a shock to an Irish person in Germany, for instance, to discover that you can't shop on Saturday afternoons. But already the writing is on the wall for this kind of restriction: shoppers in the border areas of Germany are voting with their feet, crossing the now almost non-existent frontier to shop in countries with longer opening hours.

By 2020, I believe, this will have ceased to be an issue. Shopping everywhere will be unrestricted by law, and opening hours will be determined by customer demand.

For some shops in Ireland, this will mean operating twenty-four hours, seven days a week. For others it will mean extending hours, or maybe reversing opening patterns so that shops are closed when they are now open and open when they are now closed.

It's interesting to see that changes in shopping hours are almost always a response to demand from *customers*. Retailers are often not too keen on these changes, because they may offer just the same amount of business spread over longer periods. They make obvious difficulties, too, for those who work in shops.

But despite all this, if ever there was a trend whose time is about to come then this is it: our traditional shopping hours were suited to a pattern of life that no longer exists. The customer-driven society will be one in which the customer sets the clock.

Similarly, *where* the shopping takes place will increasingly be dictated by the customer. For some products and services, *home shopping* will become the norm, as soon as the technology can be made user-friendly enough to make it an attractive proposition, rather than the obstacle race it often is now.

For other products and services, *home delivery* will come into its own again. It's very unlikely we will ever return to an era where a succession of delivery people trekked their way to a housewife's door throughout the day. But on the other hand, the practice of receiving home deliveries will certainly increase – not just of goods from the shop, but of things that previously one would have prepared at home. To revert to pizzas again, what we now see in home delivery is just the tip of a massive future business that may well transform the shape of Irish daily life in 2020.

How people shop is another variable that will certainly see change. In supermarketing, for instance, we now have a 'tradition' where people do a big weekly shop, and buy most of their needs for the coming week at one time. This is dictated to a large extent by how long fresh food will keep. It may well be that in future we will see a much greater divide between the buying of fresh food and of dry goods. Customers may well be offered economies of scale by taking certain goods at much less frequent intervals. I can see this filling a customer need if it could be married to the practicalities of household budgeting. A return to credit, perhaps? Some kind of pay-as-you-use system?

The *how* of retailing may change in an even more fundamental sense. Already we are seeing in some parts of the world an increasing tendency to regard shopping as an integral part of leisure, rather than as a household chore that has to be got over before leisure can begin. It may well be that in 2020 the worlds of leisure, eating and shopping will become totally intertwined. If that means that shopping will become more fun, I'm all for it!

Let me conclude by looking at the 2020 vision in a slightly

different way: from the perspective of Ireland as part of a European market.

I believe that in retailing terms at least, Europe will, by 2020, have come very much closer to the kind of market-place that now exists in the United States. It may take most of the period between now and 2020, but eventually the single market will become a meaningful reality in everyday life.

As so often happens, there are two contrary trends at work here at the same time. If we look at retailing in the US, what strikes you most forcibly is that in any region the market leaders are invariably regional operations, not national ones. National retailers do of course exist, and their scale is awesome, but the market leaders in each region tend to be retailers who are of that region.

This suggests that there is something about closeness to the customer that is essential to successful retailing. It suggests that local tastes and preferences can never be totally subdued, and that the most successful way of meeting those needs is for retailers not to stray too far from their local roots.

In the European context, this suggests that we will probably continue to see in each national market (including Ireland) a combination of international firms and local firms – each with their own strengths and weaknesses, and each competing like hell to serve the customer best.

Alongside that, however, is the contrary trend that is so evident already in the US. The mind-set there is to think of the country as one, as one market-place. So people do not think twice about ordering goods and services from the other side of the continent; by means of telephone ordering and overnight delivery, they can be enjoying those goods as fast and as cheaply as if they bought them next door.

In Texas recently, I received a beautifully-produced full-colour business card from someone I met. I discovered he had ordered his cards from a specialist printer in California – nearly half a continent away.

It is this concept of distance that will become a reality in Europe before long, and it presents great opportunities for Irish business. Admittedly we, in Europe, have language barriers which will always be there, but it is time we, in Ireland, saw the language issue as merely an obstacle that can and must be overcome.

The future pattern of buying and selling in Europe represents a vast opportunity for Irish companies and individual entrepreneurs. Will we take advantage of it? I hope we don't have to wait as long as 2020 to find out.

Ciarán Benson

The Arts and Culture – the Future in the Past

Ciarán Benson is chairman of the Arts Council, professor of psychology and head of department in University College Dublin.

Perhaps the best way to look forwards is to look backwards. Twenty-five years ago in 1969, the ideological battle between versions of state communism and versions of Western capitalism dominated our thinking about the world. Proxy wars waged around the globe on the backs of nationalisms and dictatorships. Vietnam became the actual and symbolic focus of self-questioning for a whole generation, especially in the United States. The Soviet Union and Eastern Europe looked forward to a long future. In Ireland the latest and bloodiest version of 'the Troubles' was beginning its twenty-five-year phase.

In the Republic we had had RTE television (a single channel in black and white reliant on individual aerials, with colour television a distant dream and video an unheard-of possibility) for just eight years. Free second-level education had been in force for about three years and grant-assisted university education had just come into effect in the autumn of 1968. The international student discontent of 1968 was felt in Ireland during 1969 when UCD, for example, had its 'Gentle Revolution'. All forms of inherited authority – parental, teachers', the universities' and third-level colleges', the churches', the state's – were being vigorously challenged and in the cultural headiness of economic boom the lethargies of the old orthodoxies were a poor match for the new oppositional consciousness. By and large it is that generation which is now in various forms of power and likely to be making decisions which will shape the coming decades, both by direct impact and as a focus of opposition for the oncoming generations.

The young Irish arts world in 1969 was very much part of this new mood. In 1966 Ireland's first Arts Centre, The Project, had started; we were rediscovering the possibilities of our traditional music, partly through the recognition given to it by people outside the country; and a new generation of Irish writers and future film-makers had just left school and were attending the universities and colleges.

What of significance for understanding the coming period from 1995 to 2020 can we identify as having happened from 1969 to 1995? The headings under which we can answer this question are those of politics, technologies and changes in patterns of expression and participation.

The political climate is now more favourable than it was in 1969 and is fuelled by a more sophisticated understanding of the argument for state support for arts and culture in a mixed economy. Audio-visual technologies (CDs, video, CDRom, multimedia, etc.) have transformed the quality of experiences of the arts, changed that quality (increased the range of private experiences and added more choice), reduced the costs and habituated the public to the rapid redundancy of technologies as new ones come on stream. The effects of increases in participation levels in second- and third-level education, together with the trend towards a common global culture, have greatly increased the numbers who avail of the arts and therefore constitute an ever-expanding market for artistic products.

POLITICAL CONTEXTS AND THE ARTS

The arts are never separate from the politics of their times nor are they neutral to them. The notion of the arts as expressions of

Olympian detachment outside the orbit of everyday life has been vigorously challenged in recent decades. Accompanying this has been the belief that the arts should not be the primary preserve of a moneyed social class but rather should be a social good available to all citizens like other social goods such as educational and health services. This raises all sorts of issues about the relationship of the public and the private sector. Take the changes in the Arts Council since 1969 as an indication of some of the changes in how Irish arts policies have evolved and the effect this is likely to have in the coming quarter century.

In 1969 the Arts Council's grant was £70,000. The Abbey Theatre received its own separate grant of £71,000, as did the Theatre Festival to the tune of £16,000. This made a total of £157,000 which in today's equivalent would be £1.347 million. The Arts Council itself seemed very much above or beyond the ferment of debate about art in society and the way forward. The idea that the Arts Council should be developing a complex policy for the arts in partnership with other agencies and that economic and social arguments for the arts should be developed, in addition to those relying on core artistic and aesthetic values, might have been treated as a pernicious and alien attitude.

In 1995 the Arts Council's grant was £16.25 million. The range of artistic activities covered by this grant and the complexity of the operation is vastly greater than it was in 1969. Much more developed also is the conception of policy-making underpinning our understanding of art and culture in societies at large. The establishment of the first Department of Arts, Culture and the Gaeltacht with its own cabinet minister was a huge step forward and places these areas of Irish life on a whole new political footing. In 1995, at the request of government, the Arts Council produced a three-year rolling plan covering the period up to the end of 1997 and costed at just over £26 million for 1997. This Plan was debated in the Dáil and received wide cross-party support. The arts and culture are now on the agenda in a way that is set to influence the next twenty-five years in all sorts of ways.

One obvious question has to do with the respective responsibilities of the public and the private sectors for the development and sustenance of the arts in a developed twenty-first century society. This is related to the second question concerning the benefits to state and business of arts support and development.

Intellectual capital, information-based technologies, cultural and entertainment products, style and marketing power will be key enterprises in the industrially advanced societies of 2020. The arts, understood in a wide sense, will be a major part of this trend. That is why they need investment now. They are the research and development domain for a whole palette of other enterprises.

IRELAND'S CULTURAL INDUSTRIES

In Ireland the concept of a 'cultural industry' has been developed over the last few years, especially in the Coopers & Lybrand report on *The Employment and Economic Significance of the Cultural Industries in Ireland* (November 1994) commissioned by a consortium of state bodies led by Temple Bar Properties. The findings of this report are of great significance for understanding how things will develop over the next twenty-five years.

The operational definition of cultural industries adopted by the study included the performing arts (theatre, dance, live and recorded music, etc.), media (film, TV, video, animation, radio, book publishing, etc.), combined arts (arts centres, festivals, etc.), visual arts and design (visual arts, illustration, photography, art galleries, applied design, etc.). Amongst the findings are the following:

- the cultural industries employ about 21,500 full-time equivalents or about 1.9% of the employed workforce.

This compares with 2% for the banking sector, 0.6% for the computer hardware industry or 7.5% for tourism;

- about half of these are employed by cultural organisations and about half work on a freelance or self-employed basis;
- the gross aggregate value of the Irish cultural industries was estimated to be about IR£441 million which is about 1.6% of GNP. This compares with about 0.8% of GNP for the computer software industry and about 6.8% of GNP for tourism;
- about 88% of income in the cultural industries is earned through direct trading activity, with about 12% being provided by grants;
- about three-quarters of that trading income is domestic and about one-quarter is export.

This is the first time that the concept of a cultural industry was empirically investigated in Ireland and, of course, it has its difficulties. Yet the findings are arresting. The contribution of the state to these cultural industries will be through the quality of its educational infrastructure, through its employment and taxation policies, through its environmental policies, and through agencies such as the Arts Council, the Heritage Council, the Film Board, RTE, etc., under the *aegis* of the Department of Arts, Culture and the Gaeltacht.

The state's contribution will be twofold: first, to sustain those aspects of the arts and of culture which are judged to be of social value but which are unsustainable without state support and second, to act as a pump-primer for cultural products (objects, activities, ideas and expertise) whose development can be profitably taken up by the private sector thereby increasing employment. To take just one example, the tourism industry is an obvious beneficiary of Ireland's artistic life and reputation, and if the market for intellectual/cultural tourism continues to expand then spin-off benefits of arts support and sponsorship of that industry should be commensurate.

CHANGING PATTERNS OF
PARTICIPATION AND EXPRESSION

Cultural democracy is currently the prevailing idea in the arts world and it is one which has huge implications for the commercial dimensions of arts production and distribution. As a governing idea of contemporary social policy in Ireland it aims to enlarge greatly the range of people in society who can actively participate in arts activity and, through educational and community projects, to develop the complex abilities which are a precondition for genuine participation. If these policies succeed this means that from a commercial point of view the potential market for services to an ever more discriminating public is likely to expand.

From the point of view of art and business in 2020 all of the above comes to depend upon emerging trends in the ways people make art, the types of art they make and the ways in which their publics engage with and participate in the work made.

We know from the national survey of the participation in the arts commissioned by the Arts Council in 1994, *The Public and the Arts*, that more people now participate in the arts in Ireland than ever before. Compared to the last set of data from 1981, attendances at arts events were up from 60% in 1981 to 78% in 1994. The survey also showed a considerable growth in the purchase of novels, plays and poetry by living Irish artists as well as of recordings of classical music.

Amateur arts activity is growing and the differences in attendance levels between urban and rural publics is diminishing. Even though there are increased levels of attendance across all social classes the gaps between the classes remain. Cinema remains the outstanding type of event that people attend, with 54% going to a mainstream film, followed by theatre at 37%.

Significantly for the social impact of technology on arts availability, the survey found that consumption of all artforms inside the home is substantially higher than outside. For instance, 89%

watch mainstream films on television or commercially rented video compared with the 54% who actually attended a mainstream film in a cinema in the last twelve months. Rock/pop music is the most commonly purchased category of art product (42%) followed by novels (35%).

Occupational class, level of education, age and region are the four key factors which were consistently found to have an independent influence on the dispositions of the different sections of the population to engage with each of the dimensions of the arts.

There is a further demographic change of note. The populations of the whole of Europe are ageing. That age group will also be the most educated elderly population in history. It follows that they should be a public for whom a taste in the arts is well developed and that therefore they should be a compelling market for quality artistic and cultural products. And the worldwide increase in population which is now growing exponentially cannot but have a major consequence for 2020 and beyond. For some this will be opportunity, for others catastrophe. Either way it is inevitable.

But Ireland's own markets are tiny; Ireland must commit itself to a strong policy of internationalising Irish arts and culture. Take for example the Irish book publishing industry. The 1995 Coopers & Lybrand report, *The Future of the Irish Book Publishing Industry*, values the total book market in the Republic at £123.1 million. Irish-published books are valued at £31.2 million (25%) but of this nearly two-thirds is accounted for by Irish-published educational books. In 1994, the total value of Irish-published exports was only £2.77 million.

Already Ireland is a strong export country in other industries. The vast EU market is likely to expand greatly by 2020 with a correspondingly large set of opportunities for cultural exports and, by way of inflow, a vast potential market for high quality cultural/intellectual tourism in Ireland itself. Availing of those opportunities means investing now; that investment should be both in Ireland and also for Ireland abroad.

Some of it should be state supported and that support should be rooted in the type of rolling planning process which has begun to be developed by *The Arts Plan 1995-1997*. This involves cooperation between many governmental and non-governmental agencies. But, critically, it involves support from the business community and not all of that support need be financial. Business generally, and not just the cultural industries, benefits from understanding how the arts work in the lives of individuals and communities. There are many parallels to be drawn, for instance, between entrepreneurs as risk-takers engaged in trying to realise often improbable possibilities and the type of work characteristic of artists. In a word, there are unexpected affinities between the artistic and the entrepreneurial imagination.

Recognising that possible affinity should be a source of interest to business and of benefit to the arts since the case for adequate state support for the arts (which in terms of the whole of current state expenditure is minuscule) would be greatly assisted by a strong, well-grounded endorsement from business and its representatives. The intricate organisation of society requires an understanding that transcends isolated and partisan sectoral positioning.

The point about attempting to envisage the future, whether it be what we personally want to achieve in five or twenty-five years or what the business of the arts will be like in 2020, is that this is less a crystal-ball gazing exercise into a world over which we have no control, and more like a challenge to ourselves as to what we would like to be the case in 2020 and whether we have the ability and energy to try and make that happen.

That means actively starting to make that future now rather than passively waiting for some distant scene change to descend upon us for good or ill. Whatever it is, it will certainly be different than we now think. That does not mean that we are out of control but only that we must continue to become the sort of society that can take the unexpected in its stride while continuing to work flexibly and adaptably for what we want.

Apart from the civic benefits of investing in the arts, there is, as I have suggested, a strong case to be made for understanding that investment as a form of cultural research and development with the state providing the initial infrastructure and business coming in at various stages of product development, marketing, manufacture and distribution. But the investment (via education and the many supports which the Arts Council and others provide to the general public in addition to those which they provide to artists) in developing the experiences of the Irish public and in extending the range of their critical abilities will be a key factor in shaping the climate of the Irish arts business world in 2020 and, by extension, the opportunities for Irish cultural business in the international arena.

NEW TECHNOLOGIES AND CONTROL

The globalisation of culture and its transworld homogenisation is likely to continue. This has all sorts of implications for issues of quality control and mass culture as well as for the challenges which are already being presented to nation states' cherished beliefs about their own autonomy and cultural jurisdiction.

The way to deal with this is not to shoot down satellite dishes but to educate citizens well so that one strengthens their powers of discrimination as active receivers of art. The globalisation process is market-driven; it follows that the best response to the fear of being over-run by mediocrity is an educated discriminating market. The Internet is a sign of things to come.

Whole new forms of communication are emerging with attendant changes in social and political organisation. This will impact on the arts and culture just as it will on other aspects of social life.

The emerging technologies will change the means by which various experiences of art are engendered; if the past is anything to go by, this will mean improvements in ease of use, in the complexity of the media, in quality, in price, in portability and in disposability.

And what of the quality of new experiences? There will be novel forms of experience such as are promised by virtual reality technologies. It is hard to say what these will be or how significant or popular they will be. I suspect that in the arts they will be new niche markets rather than revolutionary replacements for existing forms of aesthetic or artistic experiences, just as photography did not see the foretold demise of painting but rather its liberation into whole new conceptions of painting.

The possibility of new types of interaction by the audience is certainly a promise of virtual realities as is the privatisation of certain hitherto public activities such as has already occurred with music and cinema. There will be massively extended possibilities for unified worldwide simultaneous participation in artistic, cultural and political events.

However, there are qualities of experience which the new technologies will not replace but which, in my view, they will enhance, not least because they themselves will provide the foil of contrast for appreciating the distinctiveness of these older forms. Photography, as I said, did not supplant painting as was feared when the new technologies developed in the late nineteenth and early twentieth century; film did not extinguish theatre; video did not replace cinema; vinyl, tapes and CD did not replace live concerts; CDRoms will not replace non-reference types of book.

In each case the new has forced profound and valuable changes in the old, but these have generally proved to be additions and not subtractions. The entire modernist movement in painting, it could be argued, was the result of freeing painting from the need for figurative representation. The *presence* of the picture, of actors, of musicians, etc., and the often public and collective nature of the transactions between them and their publics are profoundly *social* events. This sociality coupled with the immediacy of the experience are key aspects of experience when it comes to the arts and will always be sought out by discriminating publics.

Whatever happens one thing is fairly certain: Ireland's harvest, artistic and otherwise, in 2020 will be greatly influenced by its visions and investments of the next five to ten years.

David Kingston

The World of Personal Financial Services

David Kingston is managing director of Irish Life plc, and was chairman of the Financial Services Industry Association, 1990-94.

I had the privilege of speaking recently on the subject of the next ten years in personal financial services.[1] I have now been asked to stretch my imagination to twenty-five years. That requires an approach in some ways quite different – the main influences for the next ten years are already with us, while we are not conscious yet of many of the factors that will influence us in 2020 and beyond.

Twenty-five years is a very long time. The world of 1970 was very different from that of today. Personal computers were unknown. Information access was, in general, manual. Financial services companies competed only in their own defined sector. The next twenty-five years will see even more unpredictable change.

THE PACE OF CHANGE

In a general sense, the pace of change is accelerating. The most fundamental question is whether the factors that have allowed this to happen during the last one hundred and fifty years or so, will be present in equal measure in the next twenty-five.

The two most important forces for change in my view have been the rise of a meritocracy and the availability of information.

Reading a history of Italy recently, I was impressed by the power and growth of the Italian City States in the period around 1300. What was significant was the widespread level of education – in Florence, all of the 8,000 to 10,000 children could read and write and over 10% of those went on to higher education. The brightest were educated and, to a great extent, rose to the top. Moreover the political system involved control by the large corporations with frequent change of those in official positions.

The same forces have been present in most of the Western world during the twentieth century. We have had a move towards a near-complete meritocracy, allied to an improving education system, with information increasingly available. All of this within a political system which has been relatively benign. Thus the environment has encouraged progress and has facilitated change.

Are these forces of change going to stay with us for the next twenty-five years? We do well to remember that the Italian City States did not continue to prosper in a straight line. And ultimately they became a liability when greater powers – Turkey, Spain, Austria, France, Holland, England – organised themselves effectively. Machiavelli foresaw the need for two things: internal cohesion and another factor which the city states lacked – the capacity to defend themselves against aggressors.

Are there chaotic events looming which will arrest change? In the fourteenth century, Florence suffered major setbacks due to plague and to the kings of England and Naples failing to repay loans. It is easy to see modern equivalents!

I am sure that there will be chaotic events in the next twenty-five years which will change the nature of growth, even if they do not arrest it. These events are what make the medium term unpredictable and make any predictions – particularly within a given time-scale – extremely hazardous.

This essay is based on the premise that there will not be a major halt to change in the next twenty-five years. Such events are possible, but foreseeing them is of little help in predicting the future of retail financial services. I now want to look at some other forces for change which will particularly affect financial services.

FORCES FOR CHANGE

Changing Demographics

In Ireland we boasted for some years of our young population 'half under age twenty-five' (never strictly true). Now we talk of a different world, with a birth rate down by over a third from its peak of fifteen years ago and an average family size of little more than two. Other European states face these trends in a more extreme form.

The combined trend of lower birth and mortality rates leads inexorably to an ageing population with many consequent changes. It is significant that this is still a phenomenon for a minority of countries. By contrast, Asia (with the exception of Japan) still has a rapidly growing population, as have North Africa and Central and South America.

These changes are worth a paper on their own. However, I will concentrate on some consequences which flow from a static, ageing population in the developed West, coupled with dynamic population growth in developing countries.

First of all, let us suppose the West were a closed community – ie, not affected by other countries with a different age distribution. An ageing population in a wealthy country implies a number of economic changes which affect personal financial behaviour:

- either a reduction in the working population or an extension of the retirement age. This is balanced by:
- a change in unemployment. Logically, the ageing of the population ought to reduce unemployment. Unfortunately, much of our unemployment is amongst the poorly educated who will not easily replace skilled retirees;
- a need to accumulate assets to use in old age when work

is impossible and family support is unavailable. I think it was Voltaire who said 'make savings or make children'! As this message hits home, people will increasingly worry about running out of both assets and support. This must seriously affect their financial behaviour;

▶ a desire to avoid/cater for risks such as premature cessation of work through unemployment or illness. An ageing population may also have a different attitude to risk/return.

If we add to these a world open to more dynamic emerging economies, then we also have:

▶ the possibility of much work being done by citizens of these economies – either locally or through population movement;

▶ the possibility of greater (if riskier) returns on assets being available in economies with higher growth;

▶ a growth in both economic and political power in a number of countries which are now developing.

Growing Internationalisation

We are more and more affected by what happens in other countries. The last three points of the previous section are examples of this. It is hard to believe that the trend to a more international society will change. The Uruguay round ensures more free trade; satellites ensure increasing commonality of information; capital flows are almost impossible to stop. It would take a major change in our economic systems to reverse these trends.

Countries are becoming much more economically interdependent and are increasingly sharing a common political system allied to capitalism. This does mean more movement to free capital flows with greater competition for savings and capital.

Availability of Information

Nobody is unaware of the increased availability of information. An encyclopedia on a CDRom, hundreds of TV channels, Internet, e:mail – we are in the early stages of the information revolution, another subject worth several books on its own. But what challenges does it have for personal financial services?

It is easy to imagine a brave new world of 2020 where all our personal financial affairs are available to us at the touch of a button and where all can be changed with a twitch of an eyelid. But this leaves a number of questions unanswered:

- how do we get from here to there? In particular, how do we get information from the past into the form of the future?
- how do we find new customers?
- how do we advise existing customers?
- what media are we going to use for transactions/information transfer?

I want to return to these areas of uncertainty. The one certainty is that a great deal of money will be spent in trying to find the answers to these questions.

Increasing Technology

Bill Gates of Microsoft presents us with the vision of a PC on everyone's desk. There is no doubt that technological solutions will become available at affordable prices. The power of PC networks and the facility to write systems for these networks is growing at an extraordinary rate. There seems little reason for this trend to reverse. This is bound up with information provision. It does also have a profound effect on economies of scale and on the value of an existing enterprise.

It may frequently be cheaper to start again than to adapt new technology to existing blocks of business.

This means that there are huge potential break-throughs in cost, in service and in information provision which are driven by technology. Skilled use will be vital.

A related issue is the possibility that computer technology may free more people for development (as opposed to process) work. If this is so, more people will be focused on change, thus accelerating its pace.

Role of the Corporation

Recently I was discussing the future with people now emerging from university. Many of the brightest do not see their careers with large corporations as my generation foresaw thirty years ago. Their vision is one where they develop multiple skills which they contract to the new Virtual corporation. This company has a tiny centre which contracts out almost all of its operations to those best suited to execute them.

If this is so – and I believe it is likely – then the day of the huge corporation employing hundreds of thousands of people may be dead. The world of the future may consist of centres of financial, organisational and entrepreneurial skills which employ quite small numbers of people.

Is this against the trend of market concentration and of the power of the brand name? Not necessarily – if the big names move in this direction. But I do believe that it will cause major changes in the power structure of retail financial service companies. If the successful company is one with a relatively small number of people who concentrate on a few key skills, then the rate of growth and decline of companies may become much more rapid. This implies the need for companies to become clusters of units concentrating (probably) on related but not the same tasks. In this way, they may minimise the risk of unpredictable change swamping one or more of them, while maintaining the essential flexibility of smaller units.

In this new world, companies take on a modular form. They have a consequent need to combine strategically with other companies with complementary skills. The ability to manage alliances is going to take on a new importance.

The same arguments apply to governments. Smaller units probably operating in clusters will be a better model than very large countries. In this sense, the EU and the US may be good models although some of their sub units (Germany, California) may be too big.

Role of Government

There are two models of capitalism emerging (see Michel Albert's book *Capitalisme Contre Capitalisme*). These are what may be termed the US and German versions. The former envisages minimalist state intervention and a government withdrawing from welfare provision. The latter is much more prone to state financing and to paternalistic government.

Since the US and most successful emerging economies are firmly in the minimalist camp, Western Europe must be affected by pressure to reduce social welfare. The trend is likely to be towards a society based on individualism.

This creates a gap which retail financial service providers must seek to fill.

FORCES AGAINST CHANGE

These also need to be considered, since they impact on the speed with which we must change. Some of these are:

Slowness of Learning

There is a pace at which the average person can go. This is much slower than the computer genius with an IQ of 150. With an ageing population in particular, it will take time for the habits of the average person to adjust, consequently only a proportion will – initially at least – bank by phone. This links in turn to:

Huge Investment

Many of the new technologies have high cost and a long delay on pay-off – mobile phones, cable links and fax are examples.

Only large companies – or governments – can wait for pay-back. But the evidence is of governments withdrawing from the kind of infrastructural investment which the French have made with Minitel and the TGV. Private capital looks for a fast, low-risk pay-back and this is not conducive to some of the factors for change.

Wars and their aftermaths forced government investment in research and development. Cost pressures are forcing them to withdraw. We need to put in some counterbalance.

The Past

The past is a restriction in the sense that so much has been invested that it is difficult to throw it out. Current living standards are dependent on 'old' technologies. It is no coincidence that Germany and Japan have been so successful – they started from scratch in 1945. But they are now being caught by newer developers making a fresh start.

The Unexpected

I mentioned earlier that chaotic events must be expected, whether these be the collapse of the Mexican *peso* or the war in former Yugoslavia. Events are not predictable and economic success is based on an element of chance as well as good management. This again forces us both to spread our risks and to accept that growth cannot be smooth. Chaotic events both force change and arrest it.

FINANCIAL SERVICES

I now want to turn to financial services and how they have been effected by these forces for, and inhibitors of, change. In many ways personal financial services have been less subject to change than manufacturing or retailing – or indeed corporate financial services. I do not believe that this will be true in the next twenty-five years. The forces for change I have outlined –

demography, internationalisation, information, role of the corporation – all impact at least as much on personal financial services as on any other area. Add to that the effects of deregulation and the mixture is indeed potent.

Let me look at some specific effects:

Products and Benefits

There are going to be some major changes in the need for benefits. Historically, personal financial services have been all about:

- financial transactions (moving money about);
- protection against risk;
- savings – asset accumulation;
- pensions;
- lending.

All of these are affected by the environment in which we find ourselves.

Financial Transactions

These will become much cheaper, at least in variable cost. This is going to make it easier for new entrants. It also encourages the availability of information at an economic price.

Initially, fixed costs will remain very high but they will decline rapidly unless monopolies are allowed to build up.

So by 2020 the financial transaction system is likely to have an expensive core with lots of companies using the core in their own style. It is not yet clear if profit will be maximised by developing the core or by supplying product to it.

Protection against Risk

New risks will occur and many existing risks will expand. These include the risk of expensive illnesses, of the need for long-term care, of the need for periodic retraining, of environmental hazards. Some are insurable in the traditional sense, others can be catered for only by asset accumulation and the availability of loans.

Savings and Asset Accumulation

Traditionally, people saved under the mattress or with a bank/building society for the rainy day and with an insurance company for security in old age or early death.

Savings moved away in the 1970s from being benefit-related towards inflation protection, tax avoidance and greed. We are now seeing another swing – back to a more needs/benefit-driven environment. The need for savings is becoming greater because of demographic trends, periods of unemployment, etc. Pension needs are changing fundamentally as life-time careers disappear and fixed retirement vanishes.

There is a major opportunity in a period of low inflation to provide the benefit mechanisms to answer these needs. New forms of risk spreading will be both possible and necessary for the benefit providers.

Pensions

Provision of pensions is in a sense a sub-set of savings. But in recent years it has been the accumulation of assets for a specific event – retirement at sixty or sixty-five. Demographic changes suggest that the concept of retirement is changing and movement towards a more information-based, less 'corporate' society will add to this.

Increasingly, pensions will become part of a wider scenario of income maintenance throughout life. This suggests an evolution towards private welfare provision, sitting beside – and perhaps even taking over from – national social welfare systems.

Loans

Lending is likely to become based more on intellectual assets than physical ones.

An issue running across all products is the drive towards modularity – or what can be described as 'segment of one', where customers design their own required product from a series of modular choices. This is going to mean that customers will want access to systems which allow them to create the modularity. This does not imply a universal product provider – rather it implies an opportunity for the system which can create the choice for the consumer and which can subsequently hold those choices together.

A related aspect of this modularity is the consequent shift of the customer from buying product to satisfying needs. The availability of information, products (and advice) in this new format will facilitate the switch towards needs provision. As a result, companies will have to start with customers and their needs; product creation and provision will come at the end of the process. This is a marked change from the current world where products are created first, with markets being sought second.

INTERNATIONALISATION

We have seen that asset investment is becoming more international. Personal financial services must follow. I therefore see a departure from nationally-based companies to international ones which cater for more limited niches. I think that by 2020 we will no longer have domestic markets largely catered for by domestic companies.

DISTRIBUTION AND INFORMATION

No one can access a market without distribution. Historically, personal financial services markets have been reached by using branches or sales forces, with some limited direct selling.

The availability of information must have a major effect on distribution. By 2020 information on all our transactions will be totally available to us in our houses. The winners in both the information and distribution games will be those who manage the process of getting from here to there.

Bill Gates has said that information will have to be 'engaging'. This is a fascinating point. Having the information on tap may be the easy part. The real challenge may be to provide the marketing link between the information and the customer to use a particular system. This may well be the important role of multimedia.

In this respect, the past is both an inhibition and an advantage. An inhibition in that providing information on past transactions will be very tough. An advantage because of a customer base which will be increasingly hard to build economically. I believe that the winners will be those who develop new information systems beside, rather than incorporating, the old. Equally, they will add new forms of distribution – direct mail, phones, expert systems, etc – beside existing ones. There will be occasional break-throughs like Direct Line, but I suspect that these will be exceptional.

For many years, customers will want more than one distribution form. These distributors and customers must have access to the same information. This will be an evolutionary process with discontinuities driven by cost.

COST

Personal financial services are expensive to provide. There is increasing customer resistance to matters such as:

- paying for the cost of finding one customer for every ten or twenty solicited (eg, front-loaded commissions);
- charges caused by large branch structures.

Consistent with the point raised in the previous section, we will need to keep reducing costs seen as unnecessary by the customer. The customer may pay just as much, but will want more service, whether that be information or advice.

We have eliminated much of the unnecessary cost so that we can provide these extra services. This will be a step evolutionary process – a series of moves which will radically alter our cost structures and the service we bring to customers. Increasingly that will have to be done by phone or by the customers being proactive themselves in response to marketing stimuli. This applies equally to the process of finding new customers. The ability to use technology cheaply and effectively will be vital for the successful company.

ADVICE

2020 will not see a brave new world of people sitting at home conducting their affairs with no social contact. I suspect that the need for both social contact and for advice through the maze of available information will be greater rather than less. Already, customers are saying that they want options and advice, rather than sales. Information availability offers the prospect of bridging the gap between buyer and seller.

So we will need to introduce and retain people who can really advise and interrelate. The challenge once more will be to do this in a cost-effective way – and to get the customer to pay!

REGULATION

Or is it deregulation? We have seen a steady move to deregulation in most financial services markets. Even if governments did not act, the effect of new products, distributions and technologies would bypass much of the regulation. This forces us to ask questions such as 'Who needs a bank?' or 'Who needs a life insurance company?' We need the product/benefit but not necessarily the structure.

Left to themselves, the current categories of providers would fade away and reform themselves into new types of product/benefit provider. By 2020 we might have a structure of information providers, risk takers, administrators, advisers and so on.

However, I suspect that regulation may well inhibit all of this.

This really is the great unknown – how freely will markets be allowed to operate? We have seen the effect of regulation on the UK life insurance industry. Who can predict that one or two failures in financial services will not set up the same process elsewhere?

SUMMARY

This can only be a quick sketch of some ideas of the future. I have set out to provoke with these ideas, rather than to develop them fully.

I am sure that to succeed we will need to be good at inexpensive experimentation, flexible in the speed at which we move and committed to the excitement of a different future. We will need to understand our customers' needs and to have the facility to bring new technology to bear at low cost. We will need to be able to combine personal intervention with systematic provision of customer information. Above all, we need the value set of providing real benefits to our customers whether they be the intellectuals or the unemployed.

FOOTNOTE

1. Royal Dublin Society, December 1994.

Brian Sweeney

The Promise of Technology[1]

Brian Sweeney is chairman and managing director of Siemens Ltd, chairman of Siemens Nixdorf Information Systems Ltd, and Software and Systems Engineering Ltd.

In a paper which I presented on 12 April 1991 at the Open University, Milton Keynes, on 'Information Technology in the Global Business World', I referred to an article published in the *Financial Times* on 14 March 1991 as follows:

'According to Alan Cane in the *Financial Times* (14/3/91), even as we sit here today a team of Rank Xerox researchers is avidly investigating ways in which humans and computers interact. They are looking at what is called "A second glimpse back into the future". They are in fact focusing on the next twenty years of man/machine interfacing, confident in the knowledge that their corporation had a revolutionary input in shaping the role of desk top computerisation and broadening the field of Information Technology, commencing twenty years ago.

'They are talking about an "information environment", a set of individual offices linked by a computer network which "knows" where individual researchers are and what they are doing. The technologies used are state of the art, but elementary compared with what can be expected over the next two decades.

'Each office features a video camera and microphone, a set of loudspeakers and a battery of powerful personal computers. Each staff member wears a badge which regularly emits an infra-red beacon monitored by a receiver in the ceiling. Entering a foreign office, a researcher is recognised by a system and welcomed by a computer-generated voice. Much of this research is concerned with teaching ways of enabling people to work together through a combination of audio-visual and computer-based techniques while physically separated by thousands of miles. Naturally this man/machine concept will be equally relevant to both the office and factory of the future.'

I concluded this part of the paper with the statement: 'The best that can be said is that they are at least still talking about "people" rather than globs of egghead-brain cells in carboys of nutrient goo!'

Five years have passed since then and many of the elements described above are already in daily use, eg, intensive use of PIN card access for cash, premises, telecommunications, etc, the first practical examples of multimedia, interactive broad-band communications and, of course, the first Web of the global highway.

Forecasting is hazardous at the best of times, particularly when the range is rather extreme. Periods of stability over a short-time horizon are subsequently found to be elements of the ebb and flow of a kind of harmonic oscillation, whereby fortunes, progress, prosperity and politics swing from the nadir to the zenith and back again. Civilisations have come and gone, and man's capacity to make serious attempts at regular intervals to obliterate his fellow man, while latterly possessing the means to destroy the globe, gives us pause in our efforts to predict the next twenty-five years. Nevertheless, the innate striving for a better world (however defined), continues to be the main-spring driving progress (however defined!). This gives us the confidence to visualise both incremental and radical step-type changes in the social, technological, economic and political environment in which we live. Add to that the fact that today we need to extend our vision outside of our planet Earth and cast our eyes on the cosmic system as both a challenge to be overcome and a rich potential resource for extra-terrestrial colonies, riches, technologies and, above all, mind-expanding aspirations.

It would serve little purpose to continue to speculate in a very superficial manner on the threats and opportunities posed by the above background. It is preferable to attempt to analyse how progress evolves over time in a general manner, and then to endeavour to apply a degree of extrapolation to the future of our own country. Very often the aspirations which we project today become the actuality of tomorrow. Furthermore, more than a hundred years ago, in the US, de Tocqueville observed that 'what a few do today, the many will do tomorrow'. Subsequently, in many other countries also, it has been found that the lifestyles and attitudes of the better-off groups in a society in one period can often be a good indicator of what will become the norm for the majority of the population when they become similarly well-off later.

Likewise, on an international scale, many of the consumption patterns and other characteristics displayed by people in the most economically advanced countries are subsequently replicated by people in other countries when their economies reach a similar level of development. However, in selecting a model applicable to Ireland, one runs the risk of backing the wrong horse.

In past ages the difficulty of communication, and the consequently high degree of ignorance of how foreign countries performed as regards prosperity and wealth, provided a type of arbitrage that may have slowed down the pace of aspiration. Today, all is different: real-time intercommunication on a global scale eliminates that information arbitrage and thus sets a series of challenges to be overcome by all peoples in their 'striving upwards'.

In the recent past there has been repeated reference to the concept of a river of culture – springing up, flowing, mixing, spreading in the sea, evaporating, condensing and being redistributed as a precipitation around our globe. Politics and forms of organisation in a sense follow this loose analogy, in that the totalitarian systems ultimately give way to liberal regimes after much travail along a turbulent path, only to be subsequently reformed and re-focused into the next cycle of push and pull between peripheral and central control over our destinies.

On a micro level, much the same occurs with business organisation – a sort of cellular progression – loose control gives way to centralist systems only in turn to find that the organisation may once more be atomised or reconstituted in a different form.

I hope that the above review may serve to caution any tendency towards dogmatic definition of the way forward for the next quarter century.

The fifth Technology Forecast Survey entitled 'Future Technology in Japan toward the Year 2020' is intended to be 'a comprehensive overview of future society as seen through the eyes of experts in Japan involved in research and development of various fields'. The range of the survey covers all fields of technology from basic to applied, with about 1,500 survey topics involved. This survey dates from 1992.

Similar surveys have been carried out in Germany, and if we had time there would undoubtedly be at least one doctoral thesis in evolving a comparative study of the forecasts and aspirations of the different national cultures. This, however, is not at all the intent of this essay, but exploration of some of the major topics addressed may form a simple, but by its nature imperfect, framework for a number of projections.

Against this background, it may be interesting to project some of the topics dealt with in the major study referred to above on to the tapestry of Ireland.

Looking at the factors for production – land, labour, finance and entrepreneurship – I see our major resource, both now and by the year 2020, as hinging very substantially on the labour element – labour in the form of a population that is highly educated, not only in the technologies but in a holistic manner which serves to imbue our young people with a sense of cultural belonging, while at the same time being first class as regards expertise and business acumen.

Taking this as a premise and bearing in mind that, having regard to the minuscule scale of our population and, indeed, the physical size of our country, there is clearly only one way to go, ie, to be the best supplier of niche markets – be they for physical, intellectual or conceptual products.

In looking towards the year 2020 I am unashamedly nailing my colours to the mast on the basis that excellence for Ireland will be based on the excellence of her people!

Let me explain a little what I mean.

Fortunately, there already exists irrefutable evidence that the creativity, flexibility and application of our young technocrats will allow us to measure up to the challenge to be excellent.

Therefore, intensification of the process to attract the most capable and apt undergraduates into technological fields will result in a disproportionate colonisation of those areas of activity by our engineers and scientists by the year 2020, thereby giving us a head-start on many of our competitors.

Looking at the overall European scene I assume that regardless of the number of upcoming hiccups within the EU, which will undoubtedly be exacerbated by questions of admission of new member states and the conditions pertaining thereto, Europe will proceed on a path of integration. While the degree of integration may fall far short of that of the United States, increasing economic interdependence and continuing efforts to compensate for peripherality will be sustained.

In this setting, Ireland, because of its young population – some

45% of the total being younger than twenty-five years of age – will be a remarkable reservoir of talent which can be invested to yield a disproportionate dividend to our small nation.

I have never subscribed to the hand-wringing evoked by the prospect of our sons and daughters having to emigrate in order to obtain employment commensurate with their qualifications. As a people with a fairly serious commitment to Europe and also because of a long tradition of seeking fortunes abroad, this development is not necessarily bad. The experience and confidence gained by such practice is of great value, and the incidence of returns is quite high. On this very point the future will hold far more positive aspects than heretofore. The explosion of communications, the facility to transmit voice, data and moving images will allow Virtual emigrations to take place without the emotional trauma currently experienced by parents.

Our President, Mary Robinson, has already alluded to the Irish diaspora of some seventy million people. What a wonderful force this is, if tackled through global networking so that this cultural identity and Irish roots can be levered into cohesive action to enhance the position of our nation as an economic unit. In this context, I am unashamedly committed to increased, enlightened investment in our educational system at all levels. The aspiration of education has to be that of furthering individual competencies to the level of individual attainment to exploit those competencies. This approach is far preferable to that of 'processing' young people through an educational/training machine, whereby quantity commands greater respect than quality.

The most important input to the areas offering most promise of economic success for our nation is undoubtedly that of high-calibre, highly-educated, committed young people. All about us we see the cropping by industry of temporary locations of production of varying technological complexity, from purely screwdriver operations to the highest levels of brainware sophistication. We have already seen instances of this process in operation in Ireland where what was economic to produce within our borders a few years ago is now emigrating to regions of lower wage rates. This trend seems to be irrevocable and rather than deploring this process, it is far more important to ensure that we in Ireland are at all times well qualified to take the upmarket end of production.

I have long held that the fact that the first Industrial Revolution virtually passed us by may have been a blessing in disguise. I would like to think that as a result the creative talents of our people were enhanced, particularly in the conceptual sense. I would even go so far as to suggest that this background has given us two very important pluses:

- the avoidance for the most part of the modern times type of industrial phase has given Irish people a particular talent for producing software, in that their conceptual capacity has been free from the clutter of totally routined 'deep-litter' type jobs;

- our lack of industry in the European sense – as was the case in the first six decades of this century – has resulted in our students being exposed to a deeper and wider span of theoretical studies freed from a too high degree of empirical input. This I believe has resulted in our graduates, in particular, being well-equipped to stay on the curve of evolving technology. Another factor in this context is the youth of our graduates as compared to their opposite numbers on continental Europe. The fact that we produce employable graduates at an age of about twenty-one or twenty-two years gives them a head start of three or four years in their professional lives; this is an advantage being increasingly appreciated by employers.

Thus in order to capitalise on the potential for brainware, our educational system must continue to be focused along the lines indicated above.

What do I see happening then in Ireland in the next twenty-five years?

The fundamental infrastructure to support my vision is the provision of a telecommunications system that is absolutely superb and continues to be enhanced to meet evolution in this field.

This is a *sine qua non* for the Virtual world of the future which will be realised well in advance of the year 2020. The Virtual office, Virtual factory, Virtual community, Virtual nation will happen and can only happen on the back of a broad-band, readily accessible global telecommunications network.

This will be by far the most potent factor in eliminating the actual or perceived peripherality of Ireland. Research and development at a distance from the parent company, or its major production units, has suffered from perceptions of remoteness. Education of all concerned to convince them that remoteness need no longer be a factor will be vital. I know of one recent case where the coupling of corporate R&D, with super-computer analysis facilities located a thousand kilometres away from the production plant, resulted in a new car model being introduced to the market at least six months earlier than ever achieved previously. The single determining factor was the availability of sufficient broad-band telecommunications capacity to communicate simulation images, test results and their analysis in a practically concurrent mode, thereby avoiding the consecutive approach that previously prevailed.

This type of application is really predestined for Ireland where the brainpower can be provided and accommodated in a high-quality-of-life environment with instantaneous access to all corners of the globe. Likewise the operation and control of remote manufacturing processes, which themselves can be optimally located to suit raw material supply and markets, can just as easily be effected from a location in Ireland as at the plant itself. This will bring the advantage of a high quality location at which all the necessary technological capacity can be readily brought to bear to provide the combined wisdom gleaned from an intensive centre for production remote control. In this context I have recently heard of diamond-mining taking place at sea at enormous depths, whereby the sea floor machinery is totally unmanned and process control and supervision takes place from a surface vessel. This is obviously safer and more secure than trying to man such a submarine operation. This concept of remote process and control can and will be applied to an increasing number of industrial segments based on economics as well as quality-of-life considerations.

If we look at the political situation it would appear the strong majority-type democratic blocs providing government of the nation states on a largely homogenised (real or notional) basis has run its course. The existence of coalitions of one type or another, containing in some cases extraordinary bed-fellows, indicates that a capacity to contain plurality is on the increase. Likewise, at the individual level, the striving for personalised freedom and distinctive behaviour and sense of values is very evident. Therefore, while the nation-state situation might tend to be disrupted by this trend towards more individualism, there is a simultaneous acceptance that only by belonging within an ordered social, political and economic system can the individuals' aspirations stand a chance of fulfilment. This precise situation provides scope for the Virtual community, whereby citizens of different states, but with like interests, can be accessed and cultivated as if they lived in the same neighbourhood. The power and capacity of telecommunications will allow people with a common sense of values to be interconnected on a global scale. Ireland will, of course, be part of this global village not only as regards the social and cultural value of such an evolution but also as an active participant in providing the facilities to bring this about.

My expectation is to see Ireland becoming a campus of excellence, a model society that will be the envy of larger nations. This process will be greatly facilitated by the clearly defined (small) scale of our nation. The expense and confusion that would be caused in applying this model to a larger political unit would be too complex and disruptive. Our traditions and cultural cohesiveness, which results to a great extent from our geographical insular state, will be our strength, while paradoxically the input from foreign cultures fed back from the Irish diaspora will provide the impulse for a more out-going attitude to the world at large.

The scope for pursuing the concept of such a campus is wildly exciting when viewed against the background of what will have to be made happen between now and 2020. Think of the following:

- ▶ materials: control and manipulation of structures down to atomic and molecular scale will give rise to enormously versatile and 'intelligent' materials that can be produced by a kind of genetic engineering. This type of engineering will have extraordinary spin-offs in the case of semiconductors, super-conductors, mechanical and electrical machines, aircraft, spacecraft, etc;
- ▶ chemistry: new insights into the whole area of chemical reactions such as photocatalysis will have a huge input in areas of synthesising, eg, hydrogen peroxide and hydrogen from water, and will give rise to a new type of solar chemistry in synthetic chemistry;
- ▶ life science: researches into molecular biology, cancer genes and cancer-inhibiting genes will lead to major break-throughs in the prevention, diagnosis and treatment of cancer. Continuing researches into DNA will lead to an understanding of genetic diseases. Further researches into how the human brain functions, into the thinking and learning processes, will help to revolutionise the remedial process;

- ▶ outer space: real international cooperative effort in space exploration and experimentation may well lead to the colonisation of space. What is certain is that space factories will produce exotic materials, and, of course, satellites will be developed further for telecommunications, weather forecasting (influencing) as well as for crop and traffic surveillance;
- ▶ marine science and earth science: these two segments will grow together in a global configuration to throw up an absolute plethora of food and mineral resources;
- ▶ energy: researches will eventually come up with manageable nuclear fusion as well as other means of handling dangerous nuclear waste. High efficiency, or low-cost, less efficient, solar cells will provide cheap sources of electrical energy. Relief and repair to the damaged ozone layer will be effected by recycling the by-products causing much of the problem in the first instance. Super-efficient power stations clustered with processing plants to utilise the lower-grade energy levels will achieve radical improvements in efficiencies;
- ▶ environment: data banks and continued monitoring and forecasting will allow trends and their causes to be explained and action taken to redress threatening developments. Global concepts for recycling and re-use as well as *ab initio* environmental value engineering will help to deal with current drifts towards poisoning our living environment;
- ▶ A more intelligent approach to biological insecticides will help and the development of disease-resisting crops will be a further step along the road to self preservation;
- ▶ production: new materials, new super 'intelligent' production equipment, regard for the environment on a global scale, the considerate roles to be played by human beings will lead to a more friendly regime overall;
- ▶ transportation: R&D will lead to intelligent transport

systems at reasonable cost that are self-monitoring and safe. Aircraft (or low space craft) that can deliver passengers or freight to round-the-world destinations within four or five hours will become commonplace;

▸ health and medical care: personalised electronic data storage ID cards will incorporate full medical histories, images and medications as well as real-time monitoring of potentially dangerous health conditions that will result in automatic triggering of preventive or treatment processes;

▸ The greatest break-through of all will result in the elimination or cure of such diseases as Alzheimer's. Increased knowledge regarding the immune system and the provision of a wide range of artificial organs will become commonplace;

▸ lifestyles and culture: the spin-off from many of the breakthroughs mentioned above will provide a greater facility for people to realise their ambitions regarding leisure and a sense of fulfilment.

All of the above presents a rapid course towards a kind of Utopia. Unfortunately the long history of world disorder militates against the achievement of this condition.

However, one has to emphasise the positive, and even while I am convinced that the globe as a whole can progress along the lines mentioned, the system is so large that it must allow for back eddies and cross-currents in some of the sub-systems while the system as a whole moves forward.

What a prospect the above holds for the world at large. What a prospect in particular for Ireland where we are poised and equipped in a special way to ride the wave of progress. What a challenge too to our legislators, our citizenry. What a challenge to our capacity not only to accept change but to force it in the right direction. We are talking of twenty-five years hence – 2020. When I think back to a farewell lunch I held for a very senior engineer twenty-five years ago I am somewhat daunted. This very pleasant, experienced engineer advised me then not to bother my little brain grappling with the course of prospective technological discoveries and inventions. 'We are at a technological plateau,' he said, 'the transistor has been invented, computers are in their prime, communication is going automatic, what more can you ask for?'

It is important that the number of disciples of King Canute should be minimised.

I opt for the mind-blowing vision as outlined above while not losing sight of the bliss to be enjoyed in the present.

FOOTNOTE

1. The author acknowledges the inspiration drawn from the Fifth Technology survey in writing this essay.

Pádraig Ó hUiginn

Tourism in 2020 – Managing Success

Pádraig Ó hUiginn is chairman of Bord Fáilte, chairman of the National Economic and Social Council, and former secretary of the Department of the Taoiseach, 1982-93.

When I look to how Ireland's tourism industry might develop over the next twenty-five years, I feel that the challenges of the future might best be captured in the phrase 'managing success'. We have come a long way in the *past* twenty-five years: achieving a level of success that is sometimes forgotten, but easily recalled by casting our minds back to 1970. Back then 'the Troubles' had flared in the North, and the fall-out for tourism and travel in the Republic of Ireland was felt for nearly twenty years afterwards. By the late 1980s, however, we began to experience the benefits of a programme of investment, marketing, and training to the extent that growth in the tourism industry in Ireland out-stripped that in the rest of Europe for several years in succession.

And with the outlook now for peace on our island for the first time in a generation, one can only be optimistic about the future for Irish tourism – though our optimism should not blind us to the new challenges that will arise in the near future.

In 1970, we had less than one-and-a-half million overseas visitors, while this year (1995) we are expecting almost four million. By 2000, that number could reach as high as five million. Looking beyond 2000, it would seem that before 2020 we will have to come to terms with maintaining a sustainable volume of visitors, one that contributes to the long-term viability of the Irish tourism industry – perhaps even a static volume. Hence my belief that 'managing success' will be the main tourism challenge for me and my successors in the twenty-first century.

We are, at present, a long way off 'saturation' in the Irish tourism market – however, it needs to be considered. The opportunities to increase the number of tourists coming during off-peak periods is enormous. So looking ahead to a vision of Ireland's tourism industry in 2020, I am confident that the efforts of the past twenty-five years will be seen as a necessary preparation for the well-earned successes of the next twenty-five years.

In my review below of the likely future, I want, first, to put first that future in context with reference to the role that the tourism industry now plays in Ireland; going on from there to look at some of the shaping factors that will drive tourism – and those that could hold it back; before concluding with some thoughts on what Ireland's tourism industry might look like in a quarter of a century's time.

THE FUTURE IN CONTEXT

Travel and tourism are now the world's largest industry – worth over $2 trillion per annum: with tourism alone accounting for approximately $300 billion. Not surprisingly, tourism is very important to Ireland too: the industry now turns over some £2.2 billion, while supporting some 90,000 jobs in the Irish economy. Indeed, almost 8% of employment and 7% of GNP are accounted for by the industry, and foreign exchange earnings from tourists equal about 10% of Irish exports.

Tourism, like food and agriculture, is essentially an indigenous industry. This makes it doubly important because – aside from the economic contribution that it already makes – the potential for tourism to contribute towards future job growth and wealth creation is significant. The potential contribution of tourism to the Irish economy was recognised shortly after Ireland gained independence in the 1920s. The Irish Tourism Association was formed seventy years ago and the Irish Tourist Board – a state-sponsored agency – was set up by the Irish government in 1939. This gave Ireland a head start in the field which led to the Irish Tourist Board being used as a paradigm for other national tourist boards.

Irish tourism has shown impressive growth over the past few years. The number of tourists to Ireland has grown 7% annually between 1985 and 1993. Ireland has out-performed major European destinations. Most recently, international travel by Europeans rose 1.9% in 1994 over 1993, compared with a 9.8% rise in tourist arrivals to Ireland. Looking ahead, the main objective of Ireland's tourism strategy over the period 1994-99, set out in 'The Operational Programme for Tourism', is to maximise Ireland's tourism potential by increasing tourism revenue, contributing to improved profitability in the sector and thereby creating much-needed employment.

The underlying strategy in the Programme is one that will no doubt continue to shape the development of Ireland's tourism industry in the period 2000-2020. Thus we can expect to see:

- an expansion of marketing activities, with a particular emphasis on off-season business, and on those high yield products – such as golf – where Ireland is establishing an international position of excellence;
- further product development to meet specific market deficiencies;
- an expansion in the range and scale of training to cater for anticipated employment growth, to improve the quality of service to visitors and to help the industry adapt to Ireland's changing tourism market.

To put the scale of the changes that will shape the future of our industry in context, consider that over one million additional overseas tourists will be expected to visit Ireland by the turn of the century than are visiting at present. On the basis of existing product usage, such an increase alone will require an extra 8,000 hotel beds and 5,000 hire cars (without taking account of possible expansion of the domestic market). Such are some of the features of the future that we must manage.

SHAPING FACTORS

Of course, there is a wider context again to some of the targets and trends outlined above. Ireland's industry will be shaped by many of the forces driving growth in the world's largest industry over the next twenty-five years, as well as by those having the potential to slow its growth.

Inhibiting Factors

Taking the latter category first, we should not forget that an industry like tourism is one shaped in the short-term by prevailing fashions. Thus there is an unavoidable tendency for different destinations to be considered from time to time either fashionable or unfashionable places to visit. At the moment, Ireland, and in particular Dublin, are fashionable, especially among European tourists. Italy was once such a fashionable destination, and has suffered to a certain extent from its loss of such an identity. Though, as Spain is showing, such reversals of fortunes can in turn be reversed with appropriate and timely strategies.

However, in the long run there are other, perhaps more important, factors that can work for and against a destination like Ireland. The impact of political conflict and terrorism is obviously one such factor, and one which, as I noted earlier, has affected the development of our own industry. And in today's world of twenty-four hour, on-the-spot news, the impact of images can have an extraordinary and immediate impact on would-be tourists' perceptions of one destination or another. Thus we need to be prepared as an industry for 'environmental turbulence', eg, developments such as the Gulf War, which cast a pall of uncertainty and fear over the international tourism market, even well beyond the confines of a region experiencing turmoil and conflict. We have had such shocks over the past twenty-five years and we will undoubtedly have them over the next. But as Irish tourism already begins to experience the dividends of peace in Northern Ireland, we must hope that the threat of conflict has been removed permanently from our island.

But while we can never insulate ourselves from such shocks, we can prepare for them. The future development of the Irish tourist industry will see a continuing reduction in our reliance on one or two major overseas markets, and on a highly seasonal influx of visitors. Thus we have set ourselves a target for the year 2000 whereby the share of tourists visiting during the peak summer period will have fallen from 30% of the annual total, to less than 25%. Similarly, we expect to see a higher share of visitors coming from markets that were not traditional sources of custom for Ireland (eg, Spain, Scandinavia); as well as from much further afield (eg, Japan, South-east Asia).

Of course, not all factors with the potential to inhibit growth in Ireland's and the world's tourism market are geo-political in nature. Looking far ahead to 2020, some would suggest that developments in technologies such as video conferencing and Virtual Reality will have a substantial impact on the travel market. Such a view seems reasonable given the speed of development in information and telecommunication technologies. But neither the timing nor the impact of such technologies can be certain.

Indeed, a well-known French writer, Régis Debray, has criticised some of the more outlandish forecasts for future technologies and their impact by referring to what he calls 'the jogging effect'. Citing the example of the motor car, he reminds us that many commentators in the 1950s and 1960s suggested that we would become so dependent on motor cars – and spend so much time in them – that our legs would atrophy and become useless.

But as Debray points out: people compensated for the unhealthy aspects of spending so much time in cars by spending more of their time outside of cars going jogging! Hence the fitness boom of the 1980s and 1990s.

Will we see a similar 'jogging effect' occurring as the need to travel becomes replaced with the *option* of travelling? Travelling might become something that people do as an end in itself, rather than a means to an end. Thus transforming the entire travel and tourism offer from one catering for people trying to cram in the maximum amount possible in the minimum period of time (the overnight trip, the two week summer holiday), to one designed to provide people with a richer experience, one in which they spend more time with people from local communities and perhaps more time learning about their destinations as well. A transformation that I suspect we will be well placed to cater for in Ireland.

Growth Factors

As for the factors that could contribute to growth over the next twenty-five years, among the most important of these will be affluence – as disposable incomes rise – and increased leisure time. As people in a country enjoy a rising standard of living, so their aspirations and spending preferences change and they become interested in holidaying abroad. In the 1990s, the world is witnessing an extraordinary process of rising affluence in countries as far-flung as Eastern Europe, South-east Asia and Latin America: countries that were simply not on the map, as far as Ireland's tourism was concerned, in the 1980s.

Thus we can expect to benefit over the next quarter of a century from the general rise in global standards of living. Of course, our traditional markets (Britain, the United States, Germany and France) will also enjoy rising living standards over the same period. Their preferences will also reflect the influence of affluence, though their needs will be for more specialist tourist offers such as short breaks and the eco-tourism that will be a major part of the Irish offer in decades to come.

Another key growth factor will be the continuing fall in the real cost of air fares that can be expected over the next decade as deregulation and competition open up Europe's travel market. We have already seen the contribution that lower air fares can make to destinations such as Ireland. If Europe begins to approach anything like the pattern of operation of the domestic US market, then we can expect to see many more Asian and North American visitors to Europe adding Ireland to their itinerary due to the low cost of travelling within the domestic European market. Indeed, the high fare structure between Ireland and continental Europe is still a major barrier to the kind of growth that occurred from Britain as a result of lower access fares in the mid- and late 1980s.

The View from 2020

As I made clear at the beginning, I believe that Ireland's tourism industry is poised to enjoy a prolonged period of growth and success in the decades that lie ahead.

But, of course, we cannot simply rest on our laurels. We will face many and unfamiliar challenges over the next twenty-five years. The global tourism market will become increasingly competitive as cities, regions and countries compete for their share of the world's largest industry. They will all be looking for the same things that we are: increasing tourism revenues, higher industry profits, and more jobs. Other challenges might also include the consequences of changes in the global climate, though Ireland might well be a net beneficiary from any such changes if some forecasts are to be believed!

I am nevertheless confident that we will rise to these challenges. If I were to imagine how things might look from the vantage point of 2020, I believe that we would look back over two-and-a-half decades of steady and continuous improvement in the quality and range of services on offer; and over an exciting diversification of our industry into new markets and into new product categories.

In the end, I have every confidence that our successors will look back over a quarter of a century of well-managed success.

John F Daly

A View from the Future – Dublin in 2020

John F Daly is director of ICL Computers (Ireland) Ltd,
member of the Dublin Port and Docks Board and the
Advisory Committee of the National Treasury Management Agency, and a former president of the Dublin Chamber of Commerce.

Today, in 2020, Dublin is a world-class city. Its status as the most progressive city in Europe and its strategic location make it the natural gateway linking Europe and the Americas.

The key to this success was simple – Dublin's natural advantages, and the development of a high technology-based economy. Before 1995, Dublin and its economy had not fully shaken off the traditional thinking which regarded capital and raw materials as the ways to economic success.

In 1990, over 75% of all Irish-owned industry was involved in low-tech manufacturing. Low levels of automation, high labour intensity and low value-added was the norm. Even in the 1990s, it was becoming widely accepted that technology had become the key driver in determining the competitiveness of Irish industry. Once Dublin and its leaders recognised that the city's greatest strengths were its innovative, highly educated people and its attractive environment, it quickly moved up the league table of the global economy by focusing on the support and nurturing of indigenous, knowledge-based wealth creation.

Why is Dublin in 2020 regarded as a world-class city? It is:

- ▶ an 'intelligent' city – a city which has harnessed the new technology, allowing transport, public services, telecommunications, shopping and other essential services to respond rapidly to the needs and desires of the people;

▸ a city alive with tourists – throngs of visitors from Munich to Milan bring a buzz to the streets. The National Convention Centre – built in the late nineties – has made Ireland one of the more sought-after locations on the international convention circuit. The success of the Olympic Games in 2008 confirmed Dublin's reputation on the international map;

▸ a city where high-quality jobs are available in the International Financial Services Centre and in the Dublin Science and Technology Park. These centres of excellence have contributed significantly to Dublin's status as one of Europe's leading centres for knowledge-based industries;

▸ a city with a quality of life second to none. Dublin's fun and culture, its night life, sports amenities, clean environment, education facilities and safe streets make it one of the most attractive cities in the world to work and to bring up children.

GETTING THERE

Looking back, three key features in Dublin's development can be identified: peace in Northern Ireland; getting our ground conditions right; the work of the 2010 Committee.

Peace in Northern Ireland

The end of political violence in Ireland in the mid-nineties opened the way for mature political action which brought lasting peace. This allowed, for the first time, normal economic development between both parts of the island. From 1995, the volume of cross-border business and tourism grew rapidly. The Dublin-Belfast economic corridor is now the centre of economic activity on the island.

Ground Conditions

This economic progress was assisted greatly by investing in infrastructure. Ireland's busiest route now is the motorway and high-speed rail system connecting the largest cities on the island – Dublin and Belfast. The one-hour rail journey (which includes a station at Dublin airport) makes Dublin a better choice than London for Belfast travellers flying to Europe, the US and the Far East.

Dublin's own transport network was transformed with the completion of the ring-road system. In the city, Dublin's state-of-the-art bus and light rail systems are popular, efficient and inexpensive. Removing cross-city traffic allowed the city centre and our main places of interest to be given back to the people. Most of the shopping and tourism areas are pedestrianised. No more noise, pollution, traffic congestion.

The imaginative design of the eastern section of the ring road, linking Dun Laoghaire, Dublin Port and the airport, diverted commercial traffic from residential areas and preserved the environmental beauty of the coastline. There was no longer a need for cross-town or airport-bound traffic to enter the city. Traffic headed for Dublin and Dun Laoghaire ports flows quickly, efficiently and directly to the very busy passenger and freight areas.

Dublin's ports responded rapidly to the new freedom. Implementation of technologies allowed costs to be reduced and the ports to become more customer-friendly. The removal of blockages on the UK side and the introduction of new ships on the route allowed the central sea corridor to develop as the principal artery of trade between the two islands.

Frequent, high-capacity, fast ferries now offer journeys from the UK in under ninety minutes. New international air routes have brought a huge growth in trade and tourism. Dublin continues to be a top destination for short breaks from Britain and the Continent.

Ireland's capital rapidly became a centre for imaginative and sensitive new urban architecture, serving as a magnificent counterpoint to its Georgian core.

Dublin – in keeping with its intimate scale – developed a series of urban 'villages'. First of these, of course, was the nineties development of the Temple Bar district, preserving central Dublin's remaining medieval street pattern.

Dublin now has rediscovered its lovely waterways and brought them into the daily life of the city to delight Dubliners and visitors alike. The wharf development at the old Grand Canal docks created a fishing village in the heart of the city, celebrating Dublin's reputation for seafood. Dubliners are proud of this development – good pubs, lovely restaurants, splendid seafood at popular prices.

Other precinct developments followed quickly. The imaginative development of Smithfield and adjacent areas helped to preserve the antiquity and the character of Dublin. This initiative ensured that Dublin in the 'rare old times' was preserved into the twenty-first century.

Tourism development was greatly assisted by the completion of the international convention centre in the late nineties. New events such as the spring and autumn festivals added to Dublin's attractiveness. With a new marketing drive, Dublin woke up to its enormous tourism potential. The explosion of creative energy generated by Dublin's music, film and theatre marked it as Europe's 'Fun City'.

International sporting events brought many jobs as well as increasing Dublin's tourism reputation. The hotel stock grew to match rising demand. The National Stadium built in 2000, an Olympic swimming pool, and a general upgrading of sports facilities led to our successful bid to host the Olympic Games in 2008. That, and the hosting of the 2006 European Games, has set new standards for all international events since. One in four visitors to Dublin last year came for sports-related activities. More importantly, the momentum which the hosting of the Olympics created had a galvanising effect. The shining of the world's spotlight on Dublin created a new pride in the city's development. That pride and momentum is still carried through in the ongoing improvement plan for Dublin.

The removal of the telecommunications' monopoly in 1998 and investment in information-led infrastructure kept Dublin at the leading edge of the technological revolution, and allowed Irish companies to maintain leadership in new technologies and products. This has been supported by Irish universities' strong emphasis on innovation and involvement in industrial development through commercially-driven research and development and the continuous creation of new campus companies. There is now a close association between academics and business, exemplified by the activity at the Dublin Science and Technology Park, which has become the leading centre for new jobs in knowledge-based industries.

In 1993, Irish universities attracted less than £50 million in research contracts. Today, that figure is almost £1 billion thanks in the main to the quality of resident Irish technology and engineering graduates, who, traditionally, had worked for multinational corporations in Germany and the US. The same work is now carried out on a sub-contract basis in Ireland, supported by fiscal incentives for Irish research carried out in conjunction with university research facilities.

World-class Irish companies all schedule at least one half-day a week for their managers to bring themselves up to date with the most recent technological and commercial developments relevant to their market. This is facilitated through the use of video conferencing and multimedia distance learning programs which are now a common feature of most Irish universities and third-level colleges. Specialist courses can be taken with the best authorities in a particular niche field of study, no matter where in the world they are located.

This significant change in social and political attitudes towards Irish entrepreneurs is due in no small part to ongoing educational programmes which were introduced initially into third level and a few years later into secondary educational curricula in the late nineties. In any business course taken today, there is a compulsory module on entrepreneurship which must be satisfactorily completed before a student can be awarded a degree.

This entrepreneurial drive was assisted by getting the conditions for investment right. By the year 2000 Ireland achieved a tax regime which rewarded work and supported enterprise. This required a strong commitment from government to take firm control of public expenditure and the national debt.

Their commitment was rewarded with the achievement of a standard corporate tax rate of 32%, in line with our European partners, allowing business to prosper and grow. Equally important, a personal tax rate of 25% for most earners made work more rewarding.

There was a time when this promise and prosperity was threatened by crime. Drugs were at the centre of the crime culture. The quality of city life changed greatly when the government began to act seriously on crime. The first initiative was a programme of measures specifically aimed at the drugs problem. It also introduced a criminal code in which important legal concepts were, for the first time, defined in writing. The criminal justice system became modern and efficient. An integrated series of well-focused measures – backed by popular mandate – ensured that the godfathers of crime were at last more amenable to the law and restored civic sanity.

2010 Committee

A vital factor in bringing all this about was a major initiative by the Dublin Chamber of Commerce – the 2010 Committee. In 1995 business and civic leaders came together, through the

Chamber of Commerce, to map out an integrated strategy to guide Dublin's future. A common vision and a strategic plan was adopted. The result was the 2010 Committee.

By the year 2010, this work was rewarded when Dublin was voted Europe's most progressive city by *Fortune* magazine, as a city that is vibrant, endlessly interesting and a joy to visit, a city that is unique in successfully implementing new technologies, providing job opportunities for all, while still retaining the quality of life valued by Dubliners.

DUBLIN 2020

The Future Now

Dublin 2020 is marked by three key characteristics: job opportunities are high; the city is driven by technology; Dublin's lifestyle is top quality.

Jobs

With just 5% of adults on the live register in 2020, Dublin for all practical purposes now enjoys full employment. Since the year 2000, two out of every three jobs are directly connected with or strongly influenced by the communications revolution. Most homes are now linked to Broad Band Services – giving home entertainment, home shopping, home banking. Broad Band Services have also given us access to international university degree courses.

The Science and Technology Park, opened in 1996, has attracted over fifty leading international high-tech companies to Dublin, as well as spawning many new Irish companies in knowledge-based industries – computer software, electronics, pharmaceuticals, medical products and many others.

New jobs resulting from the sunrise industries amount to 40,000. Dublin's innovative and highly skilled workforce is the key to that success, backed up by state-of-the-art infrastructure, universities and research institutions, ready access to capital and a culture which supports enterprise.

The International Financial Services Centre is now one of the world's leading offshore centres, trading daily with New York, Frankfurt, Tokyo and London.

Tourism now accounts for 60,000 jobs in Dublin – in hotels, restaurants, convention business, sports events and in the city's latest interactive science and leisure centres.

The Intelligent City

Paralleling the work of the 2010 Committee, there was a drive to develop Dublin as an intelligent, high-tech city. While all businesses and most homes were connected to the international information superhighway, Dublin itself developed unique technologies and adapted them for its own use.

The first of these was the Dublin Environmental Inventory (DEI), initiated by the Chamber of Commerce in the 1990s to fill the gap which existed in the planning and marketing structure of the city. Today, the DEI is the single computer database used by central and local government, the public utilities, and business. It works on the basis of shared information, to which all organisations contribute. Planners and developers can use it for new building schemes, transport utilities can structure their routes around it, the local authority can use it for a multiplicity of tasks – even to monitor and approve work on the city streets. It is hard to believe that a quarter of a century ago one utility would dig a hole for the simplest purposes, then tar it over in time for another to come and dig it up again the next day.

The Inventory is the standard tool to introduce new investment to the city. Potential clients and investors can be taken on a computer-generated walk through the city and answer any questions they may have regarding key indications such as employment levels, services, property valuations – even flora and fauna.

Many investors are using the Inventory as a critical tool in identifying new markets around the city.

Traffic flows have been eased, thanks to the DEI's online computer-mapping system. Commuters can now plan their routes and access real-time traffic information for all journeys, either from a home-terminal or from the car. No wonder the DEI has served as a model for cities all over the world.

The other milestone in Dublin's development as an information-led city was the introduction of the Dublin Smart Card.

The personalised card, available to all individuals for use as payment on public transport, telecommunications, admission to events, road tolls as well as shopping and banking, proved hugely successful as a safe and convenient way to carry out a variety of transactions.

The benefits to the city are immense. The information obtained from the widespread use of the cards allows utilities, retailers and service providers to tailor their services in a highly responsive way to the needs of the public. Through using information on individual travel patterns, buses, trains and the light rail service can now provide a comprehensive routing service in accordance with the changing demands of passengers. Shops can provide the range of goods, together with specialised marketing drives, to the exact requirements of shoppers. Cinemas and theatres know exactly who their audience is and what they want. Cash transactions have been cut down and the opportunity for crime reduced. The savings to the utilities and other service providers have been immense.

Commercial dynamism at Dublin port is driven by new information technology. Sophisticated cargo tracking devices allowed customers to access real-time information on the movement of their goods across seas and through the port, and to adapt their just-in-time delivery schedules accordingly.

Visitors to Dublin now find themselves entering the Information

City. The dividend from this has been more information jobs in Dublin.

Quality of Life

Above all, Dublin continues to be an attractive place to live. Rigorous enforcement of a clean air and water policy has kept Dublin well ahead of its European neighbours as an environmentally-friendly city. Improvements to water treatment and effluent plants has restored all beaches in Dublin Bay to blue flag status.

The drive against crime and drugs means that Dublin is safe for children, and it is again safe to walk the streets.

Dublin today is still Europe's youngest city. The cosmopolitan ambience generated from the tourism drive reverberates through the city. Theatres, concert venues, as well as pubs, restaurants, and sporting clubs, are the mainstay of activity in Dublin at night. There is a living pulse to the city, thanks to Dublin's international fame as an innovative, intelligent and exciting cultural city.

For decades in the twentieth century we were exporting some of our most talented people. Today, thanks to technology and the foresight of city management, we are importing work rather than exporting people. Not so many years ago, the success of Silicon Valley and the excitement which it brought in terms of technological enterprises was a wonder of its time. Dublin has become one of the showcase cities of the twenty-first century – a city which, through innovative and close cooperation between public and private sectors, education and sporting organisations, got it right ... And the best is yet to come.

Tom Byrnes

The Ides of March

Tom Byrnes is lecturer in business administration at University College Dublin Graduate School of Business, and was previously chief executive of Telecom Eireann and IBM Ireland.

It was a brisk morning, Wednesday 21 March 2020, the light was just beginning to appear on the eastern horizon. The black labrador was barely visible as he made his way up the narrow path to the summit of the hill. The light from the Kish lighthouse was still flashing in a kind of syncopated rhythm with that of the Bailey and the closer, barely noticeable, beam of the Muglins. Behind the dog the figure of a man emerged around the twist in the path. He was in his early fifties, his stride was that of an athlete, he was wearing a green and red windbreaker and a tweed cap. When he approached the summit he stopped, leaned against the wall above the old quarry and looked north across the bay to Howth.

SEÁN ON DALKEY HILL

Seán had been up since six o'clock and was doing what he had done most mornings for the past ten years. Sometimes he wondered as he looked out at the empty sea beyond the Kish how many more mornings he would be able to enjoy this time when the world seemed so full of promise and peace. He thought about the first time that he had been on Dalkey hill. He had been brought there by his father when he was only five years of age, in the summer of 1975.

In less than three months he had started school. Where did those fully packed years go? He had enjoyed school and had done well, both academically and socially. His prowess in rugby had earned him a scholarship to UCD. He got a good BComm and then went on to do the MACC. At the age of twenty-three he was a qualified chartered accountant with good prospects in his prestigious Big Five firm. In 1995 he got an offer from Microsoft and joined the firm to help them prepare for the launch of their revolutionary product, Windows 95. This product was the company's front end to the Microsoft Network that would give Microsoft customers easy access to the rapidly expanding Internet.

LOOKS OUT OVER CITY

As he looked to the north-west across the city towards the airport he could see smoke rising and being wafted in his direction by the Force 3 NNW wind. As he was dressing he had heard the early news bulletin on RTE. The struggling state radio station had informed him that there had been another night of rioting in Ballymun. Reports were disjointed as that part of the city had been a no-go area for the past ten years. It, like many of the parts of the city to the north and west, was under the rule of criminal gangs who maintained a rough justice on the principle of an eye for an eye and a tooth for a tooth.

PEACE ON THE ISLAND

Seán thought back to the great hope there had been in Ireland as the twentieth century drew to a close. The cessation of fighting in Northern Ireland the year he joined Microsoft had been followed by several years of negotiation among the various parties in the North. Eventually an agreement had been reached which for the first time in nearly a hundred years took the gun out of politics on that part of the island. The British and Irish governments had agreed to a European Defense Union mandate to oversee the disarmament of the paramilitaries. An important feature of this agreement was the decision of the Irish government to drop its long-time neutral stance and join the European Defence Organisation. It had been pointed out to the government of the day that it was inconsistent of Ireland to accept large sums of money from the EU, while at the same time refusing to contribute to its defence against the increasing threats from militant Islamic movements which were pressing ever more strongly against the EU's southern and south-eastern borders.

The sun was now above the eastern horizon and Seán realised that he had been lost in his thoughts for the best part of thirty minutes. He turned and quickly made his way back to his home on the hill above Dalkey village.

HIS HOME IS A FORTRESS

As he approached his gate he took out his multifunction communicator and entered his pass code. The small gate swung open and he entered his well-protected house. He counted himself fortunate that his employers had a policy to reimburse staff for 50% of the cost of providing electronic protection systems for their primary residence. Even though the City State of Dun Laoghaire was one of the better protected and defended areas of the country he still considered it important to have this back-up line of defence.

ECONOMIC DEVELOPMENTS

As he shaved, Seán listened to the morning news broadcast. He smiled as he thought how pundits in the 1940s had forecast that the development of TV would sound the death knell of radio. In the 1990s similar forecasts had been made for the demise of daily newspapers. Futurologists had predicted that the advent of on-demand video would, for the TV generation, lead to a rapid reduction in printed media. What they had failed to recognise was that there were places and circumstances where the printed word was still preferred to characters on a screen. True, the development of very powerful personal organisers linked to the Internet by GSM systems had given publishers the ability to offer tailored newspapers and magazines. Seán had access to several publications that kept him up to date on his business interests and pastimes. They were no longer delivered to his front door on a regular basis. They were compiled from the publishers' databases and added to the index on his home page on the World Wide Web. He could browse the index and have printed out those articles which were of interest to him. The graphics were even better than those he used to get in the slickest of magazines before the end of the last century. The Web offered him the ability to use a browser to search for articles, video and audio segments that supplemented the information contained in his tailored publications.

PRESSURE TO BUILD FORTRESS EUROPE

The news that morning had a feature on the historical basis for the development of what had been called in the late 1980s 'Fortress Europe'. It outlined how the expansion of the EU from six to twelve and then to sixteen countries had been completed by the mid-1990s. By the end of the century some countries that had been under the influence of the Soviet Union, which collapsed at the end of the 1980s, were included. Association agreements had been reached with the Baltic States, and Switzerland and Norway had maintained close coordination of their economic policies with the European Union.

In the 1990s some commentators, most notably the Anglo-French Sir James Goldsmith, had pointed out that Europe had a growing problem competing with the rapidly developing countries of Asia. His solution was to build a wall around Europe in order to protect the high social benefit, high cost European economy. His proposals were lost in the euphoria that surrounded the completion of the GATT negotiations and the establishment of the World Trade Organisation under its Italian director general. However, as the twentieth century drew to a close the economic and social pressures on European governments forced them to look again at his ideas.

AGEING POPULATION

For the last twenty years of the twentieth century the population of Europe continued to age and decline. The inclusion of the Nordic countries was to some extent balanced by the expansion that added countries from the East but demographics did not improve very much. Governments, increasingly dependent on the votes of their senior citizens, could not contemplate reducing health benefits or pensions.

STRONG MARK

In 1999 the single European currency became a reality. It was, as everyone expected, based on the Deutsche Mark. This was the final blow to the ability of European firms to compete on world markets. The cry to protect employment and the standard of living became overwhelming. In 2005 the European Union had opted out of the World Trade Organisation and erected protective barriers for its agriculture and remaining industrial firms. For the past fifteen years Europe had been steadily increasing its isolation from the world economy. The radio feature concluded with an interview with the European president, an eighty-year-old Dane, who commented that the sacrifice that Europeans had made in the past fifteen years had made it possible to assure a reasonable lifestyle for most of its by now retired citizens.

SOCIAL DEVELOPMENTS

Break-up of Families

As Seán sat down to breakfast he thought how fortunate he was that he still had his family around him. Ireland had been the last of the European countries to introduce divorce. At the time it became possible to get a divorce in Ireland it was estimated that about 5% of Irish marriages had failed. Twenty-five years later the experience was much the same as it had been in other countries that had gone down that road. Now one in five marriages were ending that way.

Cohabiting Couples

The trend that had been emerging in the late 1980s was now firmly established with up to 50% of couples living together without bothering to get married. The easy availability of contraception, and abortion if that failed, made this appear a no-penalty option to young men and women.

Single Mothers

Many women had decided that a husband was more trouble than he was worth. Irish men continued to be fond of sport and drink. Nearly 50% of the live births in urban areas were to unmarried women. The stigma attached to these children and their mothers had long since disappeared.

Growing Crime

The rapid decline in family life during the early part of the century had resulted in an increasing escalation in crime against persons and property. This was true even though unemployment had continued to decline as European firms sought young Irish people to replace their retiring workers. Successive ministers of justice in Ireland and Europe promised more police and more prisons. The cost of maintaining law and order had surpassed that of education in every country in Europe by 2010.

Middle-Class Tax Revolt

In that year the taxpayers of Ireland and several other European countries staged a revolt. They stopped paying income tax. The European government had been taking all the value-added tax generated in the Union for the past five years in order to pay for subsidies to agriculture and industry, for the cost of the health service and pensions that had become a European responsibility in 2005, and for the growing cost of protecting the Union from the Islamic threat. Instead of paying their tax to national governments, which at this stage were responsible only for education, law and order and social welfare, the middle-class areas of major cities began to use the money to develop their own no-go areas. Seán recalled how the city state of Dun Laoghaire had been one of the first independent political units to succeed in recruiting sufficient security forces to offer reasonable protection from the gangs that controlled much of the territory of what had been Dublin city and county.

POLITICAL DEVELOPMENTS

As he was finishing his breakfast Seán remembered that he had to transfer some money to his daughter who was visiting his brother in the United States. When he had been her age he too had spent a summer working there. He tried to remember what the exchange rate had been between the dollar and the Irish punt but it was over twenty-five years ago and the number just would not come to him.

Rise of Islamic Fundamentalism

Seán recalled watching a TV programme sometime in the latter years of the last century where the topic under discussion was the New Dark Ages. At first he was amused at the suggestion that the world he inhabited could be compared to the period when barbarians ruled and the only bastions of civilisation were those inside the walls of monasteries, many of them here in Ireland. As the discussion continued there had been suggestions that the breakdown of law and order that was already evident in many of the large cities of the West was an example of a new barbarism. Looking back from a perspective nearly a quarter of the way into the new century Seán felt a shiver run up his spine. After hearing the discussion he had taken a greater interest in this period of history. What the commentators on that programme had not observed was the parallel with not only the barbarian hordes from the north and east but also the growth of Islam to the south and east. Now the new barbarians were firmly in control of most of the urban landscape in Europe and the resurgent forces of Islam were pressing ever forward as they had done hundreds of years before.

What had begun as a movement of fanatics in Iran had inexorably gained support from those who saw the rapid decline in the moral foundations of the West as an opportunity to over- throw the hegemony that European nations had exercised over the Middle East ever since the dissolution of the Ottoman Empire at the beginning of the twentieth century. The ayatollahs who led this movement pointed to the destruction of millions of unborn children in a Europe that was not even replacing its own popula- tion as evidence that time was on their side. They had only to wait one generation for the will of Allah to be fulfilled.

Development of 'Europe'

The change to the single European currency was a development that in retrospect had led to tremendous changes in the European political scene. It soon became clear that the duplication of the administration of twenty health and pension schemes was just too expensive. Once the responsibility for these programmes passed to Europe the national governments were left with social welfare – which differed widely across the Union because of historical development and demographics – as well as education and maintaining law and order. The imposition of a Union-wide value-added tax to fund the above programmes and the cost of defence drastically reduced the funds available for national parliaments. The assumption of the debt of the member states by the European Treasury Management Agency further reduced the ability of these parliaments to influence the affairs of their nation.

Decline of Nation States

By 2015 national parliaments had become nothing more than talking shops populated by ageing politicians who longed for the 'good old days'. The real political power now resided in the European Commission and Parliament and in independent city states such as that of Dun Laoghaire.

Rise of City States

In the last five years these units had developed in response to the isolation middle-class people felt from Europe – less than 30% bothered to vote in the election for the European Parliament – and the fear for the safety of their children, themselves and their property.

WORLD SCENE TODAY

After breakfast Seán made his way to his office. He had been working at home for nearly twenty years now. As he entered the office his computer informed him (in his own voice) that he had mail from a college friend who was living in Singapore and his brother in the States.

Asian View of Classmate

Pat had gone to Singapore about the same time Seán joined Microsoft. He had kept in touch all these years and Seán had visited him several times. Pat's communications were always interesting. Seán called up his mail file and was greeted by Pat's friendly face and cheerful voice. He quickly filled Seán in on family news and then, not for the first time, asked Seán if he was ready yet to join him in Singapore. Once again Pat outlined the benefits of life there.

He would have an excellent standard of living. There was little crime – the rigorous way the one-party government dealt with criminals ensured that this would remain the case. Over the past twenty-five years the citizens of Singapore had continued to develop their island nation as a source of ideas and capital for the dynamic countries around them. The Chinese attachment to family had ensured that demand for education, welfare and other support from the state was moderate. Asia continued to experience rapid economic growth and even after a quarter of a century of double-digit growth China and India were still countries with vast potential.

Recently Seán had been giving more serious consideration to Pat's offer. Perhaps when the children finished their third-level education?

American View of Brother

The next item in the inbox was a communication from his brother who had gone to the United States with a Morrison Visa nearly thirty years before. He told Seán that Lucy had arrived safely and would be starting work at the beginning of April. He too had been encouraging Seán to come to the States. Microsoft had offered Seán several positions in their head office. The Americas free trade area had grown to include all the countries of Central and South America. Economic growth had been almost as good as that in Asia. The backlash that had emerged in the 1994 elections in the United States had continued well into the new century. For most of the past twenty years there had been a reaction against the moral decay which the States had experienced in the second half of the twentieth century. Church attendance was growing, the number of unwed mothers had declined substantially and the rate of broken marriages had declined from one in two to one in five – much the same as in Ireland.

Seán thought that if he did decide to leave Ireland it would probably be better to go West rather than East.

DAILY LIFE

His review of the mail finished, Seán checked his agenda for the day. He noted that his second daughter had booked the system after lunch for a review of some material she was preparing for her mid-term assessment. He knew that his son was using the other system for the next fortnight to take his qualifying exams for medical school. He would have to get all his connect time in before lunch. He must remember to print out some of the articles on his reading file. The weather forecast was good for the afternoon and he could sit in a sunny nook and read them.

Education of Children

He heard the voices of the children as they rose and prepared to meet the new day. He thought how sad it was that they had not been able to have the same social and recreational experience that he had enjoyed when he was their age. It was fortunate, in light of the state of public education, that his firm and many others had provided the products and services that made it possible for his children to get the best of education at home. The availability of good tutors in the immediate neighbourhood was also of great benefit. Because of the increasing violence associated with them, team sports were largely restricted to professionals who played in heavily guarded complexes for the benefit of those who had access to video on demand.

His Job

Seán was brought back from his thoughts by a voice message that reminded him that he had a world-wide video conference scheduled in fifteen minutes. As the manager responsible for Microsoft

Educational products, he had a lead role in the announcement of the new world network being launched by Motorola, Microsoft and GECapital. It would at last free their customers from the need to subscribe to terrestrial networks for their access to communication, education and entertainment. Developments in satellite and dish technology this century had now made it possible to have these services transmitted to their homes at a price most people could afford. It would be some time before the three European telecommunications firms that had been built up around BT, Deutsche-France and Unisource went into decline but Seán was certain that their days were numbered.

Recreation

As he prepared for his conference he noted that he was due on the tee at Powerscourt Golf Course at four. It was fortuitous that he had joined this course in 1994. The walls built in the 1800s had provided a good basis for the protection that the course needed nearly two hundred years later.

PROSPECTS FOR FUTURE

The sun was setting as Seán and his partner made their way into the clubhouse. It had been a glorious spring evening, the swing had been in the groove and the result had gone their way. As they settled into their pints, Paul, who was a teacher, began to talk about the great hope he had for the generation entering their teen years. He remarked on how they were turned off by the over-emphasis on individual rights and more interested in their duty to help make their neighbourhood and country more concerned with the needs of caring for one another. He found them very interested in the developments which had taken place in the New Christian Communities. These were islands of peace and prosperity that had modelled themselves on the monastic settlements of the early second millennium. The Internet had provided a way for these communities to interact and support each other in a wider Europe that was bogged down by bureaucratic procedures and paranoia about a resurgent Islam. He remarked that perhaps the New Dark Age would be followed, as it had been centuries before, by a period where Christian values would once again provide the foundations for European economic, social and political institutions.

Seán thought that was a very positive note on which to end a day that in the first millennium had been known as the 'Ides of March'.

Professor Dervilla MX Donnelly

The Hidden Reality?

Professor Dervilla M X Donnelly is chairman of the Custom House Docks Development Authority, professor of phyto-chemistry at University College Dublin, vice-president of the European Science Foundation, and past president of the RDS.

At the time of the accession of King George II to the throne of Great Britain and Ireland, there were many thoughtful men throughout Ireland anxious to improve the condition of their country, in particular to raise the status of the agricultural population on which prosperity so largely depended. This small band of patriotic reformers, activated by the purest and noblest motives, felt that the time had arrived at which they might unite 'in an effort to promote and improve the system of husbandry, the manufactures and useful arts of the country'. On 25 June 1731 they founded the Dublin Society, the forerunner of the Royal Dublin Society. Today, as in 1731, the attempt by Irishmen and Irishwomen to harness knowledge for the good of Ireland is still a priority and without doubt will be in the year 2020. The underlying reason for this goal is the need for employment for those who have an expectation of work.

People's lives are shaped by technical inventions and social changes resulting from research in the natural sciences and medicine. The pursuit of scholarship is an enterprise that is always moving forward. In 1876 Robert Koch discovered the causes of anthrax, tuberculosis and cholera and thus established bacteriology.

Albrecht Thaer took agriculture beyond mediaeval forms of cultivation and Justus van Liebig later founded agrochemistry. Thus medicine and agriculture created the preconditions for a rapid growth of population and an increase in food production. In 1860 Werner von Siemens identified the principle of electrodynamics and constructed the dynamo. The internal combustion engine followed the studies of Nicholaus Otto. So science always enjoyed a high reputation. Its contribution to technical and cultural development and its influence on the solution of social problems grew to be expected. Scientific and technical progress influenced the development of democratic forms of government and led to considerable freedom for the individual. However, we find ourselves approaching the end of the twentieth century with a post-modernist wind highlighting philosophy, art and literature and making short work of the idea of progress. Nevertheless, awareness of science is increasing and so greater efforts must be made to recognise the interrelationships and impact of technological development, its opportunities and its risks. Ireland dare no longer think of herself as an island – we are European.

The founding fathers of the European Communities dreamed of a Europe which would base its union on science and education, the pillars for the construction of a better future for the citizens of our continent. Greek mythology tells us that Europe was the daughter of Phoenix. Zeus was so taken with her beauty that he turned into a bull and carried her off to Crete on his back. The story of Europe is a love story with suspense.

The search for ever new hidden realities holds a fascination for man and requires a perseverance, a tenacity and a sense of responsibility for the feelings which may be opened up in the knowledge base. Today, a balance must be found between two great requirements: the pressure to extend one's knowledge and the needs of the economic system. The great need to strengthen industrial competitiveness is influencing the direction of scientific and technological research to such an extent that it is now playing a part in the education and the training mode of researchers. Neither the procedures nor the goals of research must be permitted to contradict the existing body of law and morality.

The rapidly changing landscape which is occurring as we move into a new millennium is mirrored universally in the plethora of policy papers appearing. 'Challenges and Ways Forward for the 21st Century' was a sub-title of a White Paper presented by the European Union on a medium-term strategy for growth, competitiveness and employment. One must remember that this White Paper draws in large part from the contributions of the member states. The strong public outcry in Ireland, highlighting the national neglect of science and technology, resulted in the appointment of a Science, Technology and Innovation Advisory Council (STIAC) in 1994 which has now presented to government a report interestingly entitled 'Making Knowledge Work for Us'. Hopefully a White Paper will emerge as a result of this study.

The political, economic and cultural changes are affecting the scientific community. However, it is the scientific communities themselves which are, to an extent, the cause of these upheavals. To quote Henry Kissinger, 'Technology daily outstrips the ability of our institutions to cope with truth. Our political imagination must catch up with our scientific vision.'

What kind of vision can we have for 2020? Today's technologies, informatics, telecommunications and biotechnology will no doubt be improved. But without doubt in 2020 there will be other technologies that will hold the leading position. None of us can foresee the discoveries which will be made nor the technologies to which they will give rise. It can be said with certainty that they will surprise us – the hidden reality.

The only way to be at the forefront of new technologies as they emerge is to be the master of the science in which the technology rests. Einstein conceived of the possibility of the stimulated emission of radiation as an early consequence of the new quantum theory, but we should not credit him with foreseeing the laser, nor indeed with its so successful application in surgery. Nevertheless, he started it. Lord Flowers, in a recent lecture to the European Science Foundation said, 'One can look back in search of inspiration but one is likely to be beguiled.' Like our European neighbours, the message the Irish scientists are receiving from government is to create wealth and reduce unemployment. However, it is far from clear how they want science to do that.

The science of chemistry is well placed as a creator of wealth. In Ireland the chemical and pharmaceutical sector is the third largest exporter in the state after agriculture and electronics. Exports of £2.4 billion were accounted for by pharmaceuticals and fine chemicals in 1994. Sixteen out of twenty of the world's largest pharmaceutical companies have operations in Ireland. One of the other growth areas is the food industry and chemistry is the essential science in this sector. The training required for personnel in these wealth-creating industries is the responsibility of our universities. Thus, education and training are critical elements of policy affecting society.

To attain a more highly qualified workforce governments have promoted an expansion in higher education, based on the principle of equality of opportunity and, furthermore, stipulated that science education should be more relevant to life in the community. Many questions can be asked as a result of the direction democratic governments are taking. What will be the effect on the development of student skills and social skills? What role should science play in the curriculum of the schools? A major question and a worry to academics is will this new direction cause a lowering of standards by dismissing academic skills? This last question is not totally an acceptable fear for the space created has opened doors to biotechnology, environmental studies and informatics and the special skills related to undertaking the application of science. For the higher education sector it is essential to cross the barrier of commercial exploitation of its research results. A diversity exists. Just as East and West shall never meet – so too the worlds of academia and business will remain apart. The duty of industry is to generate profits for the shareholder and its world is competitive. It is accepted that the profits generated are for private gain and may or may not benefit society. The concept of public good does not necessarily concern industry. On the other hand a university or higher education institute is bound by its structure to generate knowledge, preferably through collaboration between scholars, for the good of the human race. The fundamental differences must be recognised and respected otherwise conflict will ensure. The real challenge is to find a mechanism which allows the economy to benefit from the commercialisation of new knowledge while appreciating and recognising the legitimacy of the different standpoints.

Science, technology and innovation go hand in hand and these have been linked more recently with the word 'foresight', which is on the lips of many science policy mandarins. The big question is can foresight increase innovation sufficiently to overcome the problems of unemployment? The key to foresight is participation. The idea is to gain the views of as many people as possible in as many different areas as possible – industrial managers, researchers, scientists, managers in the public services, policy-makers, etc. The challenge then is to marry what the researchers regard as possible with what the users of research regard as desirable. The result of this data collecting is to aim at prioritising. B Martin and J Irvine in *Research Foresight: Priority Setting in Science* (Pinter, 1989) have summarised the foresight programme as the five 'Cs' – Communication, that is bringing together people in a novel form in which they can interact, Concentration, Coordination, Consensus and Commitment. Will foresight procedures succeed?

Our attention has been drawn by Philippe Montigny, at the Ciba Foundation Conference on the evaluation of scientific research in 1989, to what has become known as the 'Cassandra Paradox'. This analogy is worth considering as the foresight programme begins to produce results. In Greek mythology Cassandra was blessed with the gift of prophecy but was also cursed with an inability to convince anyone of her predictive skills. She forewarned her father about the fall of Troy but was unable to convince him to believe her and to act to prevent it. The problems for Cassandra were threefold. She lacked legitimacy, she was supposed to learn from her father, not vice versa. She was not competent. She was female in the days when the military was a wholly male sphere and she had no authority. Had she been a priestess of Delphi, one way in which a female could influence, she might have had more persuasive success. Legitimacy, competence and authority can therefore be considered the three most important qualities needed by the organisers of foresight programmes. Time will tell if those advisers in the foresight programme are more successful than Cassandra.

In the wake of all the large-scale political debates on the future of research, one must not forget that the public attitude to science is changing. In many respects the public in industrialised countries is more familiar with science and more demanding. But the same public shows a wariness of the products of scientific research, eg, nuclear power and genetic engineering. It is against this background that science needs to explain its contribution to social well-being and economic growth. This subject is debated in all European countries without exception: 'Never before have so many people been dependent on the scientific actions of the individual. Never before has the individual researcher been as powerless in the face of the process of science,' stated Wolfgang Frühwald, President of the German Research Council (DFG) in a Trinity 400 Lecture in 1992.

Evidence is clear that research and development should be left to the market to decide. The significance of the information technology revolution is that it has shifted power into the hands of the consumer and away from the industrial producer. The impact of altering demographics on the customer base and, in particular, the maturing of society is playing a major part in decision-making. The belief that information technology, a revolution that has taken place in the last decade, would be the magic key which would provide the desired transformation of dross into gold must be questioned. By informing companies about customers' needs and customers about available products the information revolution would help to reduce the wastage of developed products. Scientists all too often forget that there might be little demand for their products at the price at which they could be produced. In these circumstances scientists are deluding themselves if they blame industry or government for failing to extract marketable technology from research.

Lovers of Lewis Carroll's *Alice in Wonderland* will remember the moving scene in which the Walrus and the Carpenter invite some oysters for a walk along the beach with a view to making a meal of them. To distract their attention from this ambition, the Walrus addresses them:

> 'The time has come,' the Walrus said
> 'To talk of many things:
> of shoes – and ships – and sealing wax –
> of cabbages and kings –
> of why the sea is boiling hot –
> and whether pigs have wings.'

The Walrus might have saved his breath by telling the oysters that the time had now come to discuss a number of topics of empirical observation and certain problems arising out of them.

The communal nature of scientific research is a feature of modern times and individual scientists are slowly giving way to teams. The team is now giving way to the network and these networks are electronically linked by ever more sophisticated technologies. Networks allow expertise to spread across continents. What is the potential of this development? Mainly that of international collaboration which before might have required years of negotiation at the level of policy-makers and which can now be carried out in an informal fashion. There is a greater opportunity for international partnership, for informal exchanges and a very rapid method of invitation to collaborate amongst leading laboratories. The term 'cluster' is now appearing regularly in the scientific journals. Geography no longer plays a part in the activities of scientists.

The benefits of an international approach to basic research have been accepted by Europe. International organisations have a responsibility in this area. We are now on the Fourth Framework programme which is coordinated by the European Commission. The Commission demands and is responsible for a high standard of excellence as well as fairness in terms of national distribution of public funds.

Among scientists there is a natural rivalry for excellence. Europe is a rich and prosperous region with a large share of the world's best scientific brains. 'The European choice of priority research areas cannot but take into account the multiplicity of needs expressed by a complex socio-economic system with its long scientific and industrial tradition and strong environmental constraints.' Thus stated Umberto Colombo, former head of ENEA – the Italian energy research organisation – in his recent speech at 'Choices for Europe', a symposium held in The Hague in February 1995. Europe cannot afford to neglect leading-edge technologies at the frontier of human knowledge which will determine major developments for the foreseeable future. The

European report on science and technology indicators (EUR 15897 EU) makes fascinating reading.

Of one thing I am certain, the course of basic research is being wrongly influenced by hopes of early gain. Among the many areas in science that need to be researched are:

- oxide crystals; the chemistry of fullerene, dendrimers, and other molecular materials, to construct molecules with microproperties to determine macro behaviour;
- in life sciences understanding the immune system, the nervous system, plant defence mechanisms and photosynthesis;
- the domain of complexity, including non-linear dynamics, deterministic chaos, non-equilibrium thermodynamics, operating across a wide range of applications, from meteorology to climate research, from unstable phenomena to organisational processes;
- nanotechnologies and the construction of electronic, optronic, mechanical components;
- artificial intelligence, with the development of neuronal chips and computers, android robots, artificial life forms;
- mathematics, a subject whose strategic value in areas such as speech therapy, numerical analysis, discrete mathematics, the mathematics of uncertainty and discontinuity is now appreciated.

Hidden in these sciences are the technologies of 2020.

An interesting global trend is occurring, notably in the pharmaceutical industry, which will offer good opportunities for universities in Ireland. Because of the rapid pace of new product development less and less basic and strategic work is being carried out by industry. As stated by G T Wrixon, the Director of the National Microelectronics Research Centre, in his recent Boole lecture, 'If innovation is to continue at its present pace the research will have to be carried out somewhere and more and more industry is coming to the conclusion that the correct place for this to happen is not in their own R&D laboratories but in university laboratories. This is even more so for the pharmaceutical industry in Ireland, in particular for our relatively small indigenous industries as well. Apart from new product development I do not see industry in Ireland having the capability nor indeed the inclination to carry out the applied strategic, not to mind basic, research in science and technology necessary to support their product innovation.'

In science all rational human faculties come together. Science is not only knowledge in the hands of scientists, it is the research and teaching, inventing and solving of problems, the planning and the criticisms. Science in progress represents the eternal youth of the scientific mind. What allows it to grow old according to Jürgen Mittelstrass, professor of philosophy at the University of Konstanz, is 'dogmatism and a world that no longer trusts in or has become tired of its innovative power and seeks to return to myths'. This applies not only to the natural sciences but also to the social sciences and to the humanities. The social sciences are not irrevocably wedded to the present which they seek empirically to comprehend, nor are the humanities wedded to the past which they seek to interpret. Judging by the problems of the natural sciences, the social sciences and the humanities must think of something new as well. As Mittelstrass says: 'If they offer only the fleeting present and the mild afterglow of the past then the distance between the natural sciences, the humanities and social sciences will become ever greater.'

Tony Barry

A Construction Industry Perspective

Tony Barry is chairman of CRH plc, director of Greencore
plc, of DDC plc, and the court of the Bank of Ireland.

To look five years ahead and forecast with confidence in a
business planning sense is dangerous. To attempt it for twenty-five
years is a pure crystal ball operation. Nonetheless I can speculate
and know that I will not be held accountable if the outcome does
not match my predictions.

The only business I know in depth is the construction industry
and in particular the building materials side of it – having worked
for CRH plc for over thirty years at virtually all levels. In that sense
I can look back to say 1970 and try to draw parallels between
how we saw the future of the industry then and what has actually
happened over the twenty-five years.

At that time the Western world was still pursuing the ambitions
for society that emerged after World War II. This was being done
in a competitive situation between two economic systems –
communism and free enterprise capitalism. Each aimed to provide all of its citizens with good shelter, good food, health,
education and the opportunity to pursue happiness – whatever
that might mean in either case. The construction industry participated hugely in this drive forward of humanity – and some of the
worst excesses of what happened in the first twenty-five years
after World War II and, to some extent, in subsequent years in the
seventies are still with us today. This is more evident in the Eastern

bloc countries, which attempted the 'great leap forward' under the communist system, than it is in the West. Rigidities of the system operated against adaptation to changing needs, dictated by the effects growth was having on life quality and resource usage. Nowhere was this more evident than in the environment and the infrastructure of roads, building, water and power supplies, sewage treatment systems and transport networks. High-rise buildings were the solution for mass shelter and they have failed under virtually all criteria on which they can be judged – aesthetic, structural, inbuilt obsolescence, and in human living terms. Some of the industrial development was positively dreadful in terms of pollution control.

The drive to put a car at the disposal of at least every family led to traffic chaos and widespread road building, often conducted with little consideration for the countryside or the heritage of the towns and villages ostensibly to be served by the network. Water to every house was not accompanied by collection systems for waste water that adequately treated and returned it to the rivers and sea at acceptable quality. Heating of all buildings and the provision of light and energy to workplaces and homes resulted in often ghastly networks of poles and cables. TV and radio antennae 'blossomed' everywhere. The convenience and pleasure of fridges, dishwashers, music centres and TV was accepted without consideration of how the frequent obsolescence of the equipment was going to be dealt with – never mind the packaging that went with it!

Those years were ones of continued growth for the industry – 5% compound was the order of the day. We participated fully seeing a doubling of volumes almost every decade. Indeed the whole thrust of planning the future for the industry was how could the materials of steel, aluminium, cement, aggregates, clay, timber, glass, plastics, etc, be made and supplied into the future on the basis of the huge increases in demand prophesied. Also, where was all of the skilled labour to come from to build what was needed, even if all the products could be manufactured?

The first oil shock of 1973 brought growth to a halt. It resumed in the mid-seventies only to be stopped once again in the 1979 oil crisis. Poorly thought-through fiscal and monetary policies to cope with the situation resulted in huge inflation. Meanwhile energy producers switched massively to coal and nuclear power and the North Sea developments reduced dependence on Middle East oil. The building industry believed that a low energy require-ment in building was going to be the most important criterion for the future and much thought and research went into a range of possible solutions. We in CRH believed that our basic heavy materials of block and concrete would be replaced in the long run by lighter materials with high insulation values, eg, timber, various composite boards and panels, etc.

The future did not work out as predicted:

- ▶ oil went into surplus with the switch to coal, gas, etc, and the price came down in real and indeed in nominal terms!
- ▶ supplies of oil today are still as high as they were in 1973 when it was predicted we should have run out by the year 2000!
- ▶ new materials did not supplant the 'traditional' to any significant extent; designers and users had become scep-tical and uneasy about durability and performance over many decades. Kipling's rhyme still seemed to hold good: 'How very little, since things were made,/Things have altered in the building trade.'

The inorganic materials of the earth will continue to be the prime source of building's basic components.

What lessons have we learnt in the past twenty-five years that will help us get a more accurate fix on the next twenty-five? I suppose the first basic is that apocalypse or paradise are unlikely – unless by divine intervention or the blind stupidity of humankind. The latter may be the more likely of these very outside possibilities. In the building industry we can look forward to intense participation if we exclude these two possibilities. The past fifty post-war years saw basic technology being harnessed almost insensitively and blindly to fulfil our needs of shelter, consumption, travel, health and entertainment. The last twenty-five years of this fifty saw a gradual awareness and comprehension, particularly in the democratic West, that massive change in a short time creates massive and unwelcome complications. The great thrust of humanity for a better life for all has sobering implications if it is to be achieved in a short time.

It is salutary and indeed almost comforting to reflect that here in Ireland particularly, business, ie, private as opposed to public business, has if anything a higher and better profile than it did have. Governments and state power are no longer seen as the source of solutions to problems – perhaps it is even the reverse. The ability of state institutions to deliver effective, quality and low-cost products and services is no longer believed in, least of all by the state itself. This gives rise to a great challenge for the private sector – and also imposes a great responsibility. These macro changes in society have major significance for industry and indeed for the construction industry. It is not a case of the state 'withering away' in Marx's words – rather it is a case of reverting to the role of regulator and provider of services such as infrastructure, security and social welfare and leaving the rest to private initiative. It has been the experience of the construction industry that the state intervention to pump-prime the economy through this route has accentuated business cycles with often very bad effect, particularly in the 1978-80 era. This re-balancing between the public and private sectors was certainly not foreseen twenty-five years ago.

Within the construction industry another trend that has become very clear in the past two decades has been the relative growth in the repair, maintenance and improvement sector versus primary greenfield construction. This is particularly so in the developed Western world where the percentage of total spend in this area generally exceeds 50%. The post-war era saw a demand for new roads, new houses, new factories, new farm buildings, new hospitals, new schools. All of these structures wear out or become obsolete and have to be adapted to changing needs, hence the growth in this sector. This is set to continue and grow even further.

This is the era of information technology, of instant communication and mass access to knowledge. What change has this wrought in our industry? In particular CAD/CAM technology and automation has greatly enhanced the industry's ability to plan and control more effectively and to enhance quality and reduce the cost of products. The basic products have not fundamentally changed but their fitness for their purpose has hugely improved. An example of this is the basic concrete block. In the past two decades its cost in real terms has almost halved; it is significantly more accurately sized; it is made with less energy and waste; and it is delivered to the mason packaged and by crane precisely where it is needed. The same is true for many other products in the industry.

Given the background I have sketched for the period since World War II and in particular for developments in the past twenty-five years, what can business and, in particular, the construction industry expect in the next twenty-five years? Will social, political and/or economic changes fundamentally affect our future? I prefer to take a positive and constructive view of the future and to hope that governments will learn better to govern; that business will be about the long term and more ethical; that the media will become more responsible and less trite and divisive; that crime and drug abuse will reverse in direction; and that personal responsibility, dignity and some belief in the future will again become the norm.

If these trends are re-established then our industry will have a good future and one where those in the business will reinvest much of the profits. The products will not dramatically change. We will still be using stone, reformed stone by way of concrete, clay products, glass, timber, aluminium, steel, copper, etc. In other words reshaping the products of the earth as the industry always did. We will extract with more care for the environment and restore in an attractive and properly landscaped manner. We will make the products with less energy and waste and recycle as many of them as is practical and economic.

The buildings we construct will be more aesthetically pleasing and more in conformity with their natural surroundings. They will be energy efficient, quiet and healthy and designed to allow for change or for a finite life. Our roads will be quieter, cars will be more energy efficient and safer and towns and cities will again become pleasant for the pedestrian and cyclist. People will have enough individual space and occupation to satisfy their individual needs and will have the liberty and capacity to create their own immediate environment – with help from the industry, of course! These things are all happening now, in gradual and, at times, in difficult and tortuous ways. All of this, of course, is to a degree wishful thinking and some 'bolt from the blue' may change life utterly either temporarily but seriously, or worse still, permanently. We tend to forecast sudden shifts as having dramatically bad effects rather than good.

Of the present threats to the future twenty-five years which might seriously affect progress I would rate them as follows:

- natural resource needs: can be managed for probably most scenarios;
- serious global warming: if as a result of human actions, can be managed; not likely within the time-scale;
- social and political order: is and will be the most difficult area and hopefully only the source of local as opposed to global shocks;

- health care and ageing process: sucking in too much of developed economy's growth and savings, the choices and solutions will be painful in human terms; it is disturbing, to say the least, to have, perhaps, to play off the past against the future;
- education, training and child care: more crucial than it ever was and more uncertain as to policy and social mores. IT technology, computers, Internet, etc, will never be a full substitute for individual human guidance and interaction.

My prediction in short is that the future is in our own hands, and that with our present technologies and understanding of our planet, business will cope and life should be better for most – but it will not be achieved without hard work, some sacrifice, prudent risk-taking and the maximum use of reason. It is said that people living two hundred or even a hundred years ago would not recognise today's world. They certainly would be amazed at many developments but would I think find human nature not too different.

People at the autumn of their lives forty or fifty years ago thought that technological developments had peaked. Land, sea and air had been conquered by man and machine as had all forms of production.

Fundamental technology has not changed in many fields but it has moved forward steadily in a more focused and refined way. There has been a huge increase in the understanding of how humans and the world work and interface with each other. As this knowledge grows the combined effects of advances in different areas will lead to dramatic changes in many areas – information sourcing, analytic aids, further automation of mass production, pollution control, food production, etc. Yes, great changes there will be, but old Adam and Eve will not be greatly altered – nor will the houses they live in.

John Dunne

Intriguing Prospects

John Dunne is director general of the Irish Business and
Employers Confederation (IBEC), member of the National
Economic and Social Council, the Central Review Commit-
tee and the Executive Committee of UNICE (the Confed-
eration of European Industry and Employers
Organisations).

> *Change is inevitable.*
> *In a progressive country, change is constant.*
> **BENJAMIN DISRAELI, 1867**

PREDICTING

The only way we can make a stab at predicting anything is to look
at what went before and try to draw a line from the past through
the present to the future. Yet this sort of straightforward use of our
analytical skills just will not work when we try to look at how our
society will develop from here. The sheer rate of change is such
that most of us now regard this 'turbulence' as an ongoing part of
our lives. All we can draw from our past is that our future will be
unrecognisable.

Yet look at what doesn't change. In all societies, at all times,
business is about selling things that people want at prices they
find attractive. Dress it up as you will, the finances of an individual, a company, a nation, or a trading bloc essentially come down
to that. In these pages I will apply this straightforward maxim to
show how Ireland has very good reason to be optimistic. It is
largely a matter of attitude whether we regard the turbulent seas
ahead as threats or opportunities. I want to look at some of the

things that are happening now and suggest how we can harness them to Ireland's advantage.

BIGGER STAGE

We know that these basic rules will be played in future on a bigger and more open stage.

Since the end of World War II, there has been a steady movement among nations to develop into larger trading blocs. Ravaged by war, Europe was determined to be self-sufficient in steel and food. So began the structures which have evolved into the wider European Union. Similar blocs are developing in North and South America, the Far East and, possibly, Africa and Asia. The next major changes will come when new major players – such as China and India – come fully onto the world economic scene.

These are countries that will, of course, compete for markets but they are also customers. We know – we know now – that competition for investment and for the sale of products will intensify. We also know that the growing emergence of vast numbers of customers at a time of globalisation will undoubtedly have a dynamic effect. Of course, there will be pressure on certain sectors but the overall benefits for an open trading economy such as Ireland's can, in the long term, be positive. They will be positive if we have the courage to fully understand the competitive challenges and to take the necessary measures to adapt to them. As I said – attitude.

Just as nations forged links to create trading blocs, so the blocs themselves have recognised the mutual value of establishing open trading relationships; the recent GATT agreement was a major link in this play of global politics.

A TRANSFORMED SOCIETY

Ireland's Industrial Revolution is quite recent. Over the last generation we have seen the rapid movement from being largely agrarian to being a complex, pluralistic society. In the language of politics, there is no constituency in Ireland that is 'rural'. In the language of marketing, there are vastly more ABC1 and C2DE customers in every corner of the land than there are F1 and F2 consumers. In every county in Ireland a majority of workers are on PAYE. The kids follow the ups and downs of UK or European soccer clubs while the parents know more about the characters on TV soap operas than they do about their own neighbours.

These social changes follow from economic changes. Our behaviour is a direct consequence of our transformation of ourselves into a developed economy. Through deliberate action over the last quarter century or so we have attracted a significant body of foreign investment and this has had major effects on our industrial development. Now while it is true that in some sectors in Ireland the activities engaged in remain too far down the added-value chain, there are others where developments are extremely exciting.

There has, of course, been pain along the way. Many of our traditional sectors have been rationalised to an almost unrecognisable extent – in quite a number of cases out of existence altogether. Many of those that survived are finding life extremely tough as they struggle in a world where global competition has stood traditional notions upside down and where only the leanest and fittest can survive. There are, though, many Irish enterprises which themselves are extremely lean and fit and, in the process, have become world players in their own right. These efficient, dynamic companies show just what can be done and are a valuable encouragement to others to face up to the future with the optimism that will be necessary.

OPTIMISM

Ireland has every right to be optimistic. As this contribution is penned, Ireland's standard of living continues to converge with that of mainland Europe. It is now at 85% of the European average and will reach parity by the end of the century. (That is if we measure national wealth in conventional terms. Along with J K Galbraith, we should recognise the limits of GNP as a measurement of the real quality of life.)

WORK

Tempering this optimism is the unacceptably high level of unemployment. It would be unfair to ourselves not to recognise that progress has been made. Over the last years in particular the number of people at work has increased steadily. Our considerable achievements in increasing the numbers at work have been overshadowed in the public mind by the monthly statistic on the Live Register of Unemployed. What is forgotten is that an economic miracle would have been needed to generate the employment necessary to cater for the tens of thousands of young people entering the labour market. The demographic shape of Irish society – with its young population bulge – would have constituted an insuperable problem irrespective of how we had managed our resources over the past quarter-century although, of course, we could – and should – have done considerably better. The fact remains, though, that we have increased numbers at work. As the population bulge passes along and as participation rates level off, the sense of crisis should begin to reduce. Facing an extraordinary challenge over recent decades, we have at least shown that progress is possible.

It is difficult to talk in convincing terms of what the future will hold for employment but we know that we have had the fortitude to tackle enormous obstacles in the past. We must continue to keep our eyes fixed on the basic business of selling our goods and service – recognising the competitive pressures inherent in this process – and then see how to make best use of Ireland's unique characteristics.

There are those who react to each new technological innovation as a threat. I remain convinced that for a society – just as for an individual – technology offers increasing degrees of freedom. It is not that we have our backs against the wall, it is rather that we have never faced such an open sea.

WORK ORGANISATION

The organisation of work is changing fundamentally. In broad terms it seems increasingly likely that – apart from those aspects of manufacturing that will continue to require set-piece delivery – there will be a considerable break-up in the way in which work is currently structured. Increasing numbers of people will work from their own bases, in many cases from home, either as employees or as self-employed. Technology – and the new social structures which accompany this technology – will allow them to link into the system through appropriate information technology (IT) mechanisms.

The rocket fuel behind this fundamental societal change is technological innovation, itself fuelled by investment in research and development (R&D). Grasping the freedom which such technology can offer, individuals will choose to restructure their lives. Imaginative employers will use the technology to minimise their own costs while maximising the quality of life for themselves and their employees.

While this is happening in this part of the world, the trend for the transfer of low-technology production to parts of the world with large labour surpluses, and therefore cheaper production costs, will continue. This will pose problems for those developed countries like Ireland which also have large employment surpluses but which are not low cost. For them, the case of a competitive commercial environment for large-scale investment in R&D is even more acute.

So where does Ireland have special advantages? Well, just look at the sort of society we are. The pluses are that we are young, well-trained, a nation state within the European Union whose environment is comparatively unspoilt for a developed country and whose industrial revolution is but a quarter-century old. The main negative is our peripherality.

Across the globe developments in the services sector are likely to be even more far-reaching than those in industry. Ireland, for the reasons given above, is well placed to benefit from this generation of wealth. Already we have a glimpse of what is to come. The combination of the explosion in information technology and similar developments in telecommunications is revolutionising a range of our activities in diverse areas such as banking and other financial services, retailing, entertainment, leisure, domestic administration, to mention just a few.

The tourist industry will expand to undreamed-of levels. Developments in transport, increases in consumer spending power, improvements in infrastructure and political stability worldwide, will boost tourism globally. Again, Ireland is well placed to make disproportionate gains.

Some of these changes will simply impose themselves, requiring adaptations that will be fairly standard throughout the world. Others, for example in the tourist industry, will require quite specific responses depending on the type of development favoured by individual countries. For us, the case for placing our interests in the 'high-value' quartile seems compelling.

POLITICAL AND ECONOMIC STABILITY

Although at the time of writing the tragic war in the former Yugoslavia continues unabated, and a number of regional conflicts continue, there is – by any historical comparison – global stability. While the risk of localised turbulence remains, there seems to be a reasonable chance that the comparative peace we now enjoy will continue.

The freeing-up of world trade, the establishment of the World Trade Organisation, and technological development, are all helping in the conception and production of new products for markets at a breathtaking pace.

Given the emergence of India and China as economies with disposable consumer income, it is at least arguable that buoyancy in world trade – in which I include the service sector and especially tourism – will significantly offset the loss of jobs in manufacturing caused by the rapid rate of technological change.

CHANGES WITHIN STRUCTURED EMPLOYMENT

There is likely to be continuing pressure for change for those in so-called 'structured employment'. In the developed countries there will be more skills required, more education, more opportunity for more individual decision-making. All these developments will increase the momentum towards less regimentation, more involvement, less reliance on traditional mechanisms. There may well be a natural movement against trade union membership arising simply from the organisation of work. The trade union movement will need to reassess its current rationale if it is to survive. (In Ireland it is obvious that the process of reassessment has already begun.)

Increasing competitive pressures will also affect the labour market. In Europe, at least, it is likely that long-standing traditions will be sufficiently strong to ensure that adequate social protection remains. Labour market initiatives will keep up sufficiently with changing demographics and new competitive requirements to ensure that the difficult circles, which will always have to be squared, continue to be successfully negotiated.

Equally, there will be changes – changes which I optimistically believe will be welcomed by everyone. On the one hand these will lead to less regulation, more self-reliance and will thereby respond to a need for self-respect and competitive realities. On the other hand, they will respond to the needs of the less fortunate in our society.

Unfortunately, there is some evidence of an alienation of too many young people from the world of business – and not just from what we know as 'organised' business. This is a self-indulgence that we cannot afford. Ireland urgently needs the development of an entrepreneurial culture. Selling our goods and services, seizing the opportunities offered by technology, all this is dependent on – attitude.

The situation regarding unemployment – at least in developed countries – may in the longer term be less negative than some commentators now believe. As has already been indicated it is likely that there will be greater equilibrium in participation rates in the labour market and the changing demographics will play a significant role. For the developed countries then the challenge is more likely to be a competitive one and the response to it is increasingly likely to be found in further technological development, education, skills development, a deepening of investment in R&D and innovation, and newly-focused vocational training.

EDUCATION

It is clear that the nature of employment is changing and will continue to do so. Even within the industrial sectors there will be fewer and fewer completely unskilled jobs. The organisation of work too will change with the trend towards team working accelerating in a variety of new forms. All these developments will put further pressure on education and training. At other stages of our economic development we have seen the problems caused by a mis-match in education/skill attainments and job requirement. Some of our labour market initiatives – in both vocational training and in the development of some higher-level skills – are misplaced. For too long the important areas have been supply-driven and there is a clear necessity to correct this mis-match.

Ireland will benefit directly from more business education link-
ages and more involvement of business in the development of
training initiatives. Greater participation by business in these vital
areas is likely to be a significant feature of the future. A *sine qua
non* is a real recognition by business of the value of significant
investment in education and training and a recognition that while
a new emphasis is needed, it should not be at the expense of
providing a sound intellectual basis for future specialisation.
There will, however, be a clear need for such specialisation on a
research-driven basis – matching needs and appropriate skills to
an increasing extent.

Some may argue that education and training are public policy
issues alone but business needs to influence the agenda. For too
long business has been a passive recipient of the products of the
educational system. This will no longer do. However, nobody
should argue that our education should be narrowly or techni-
cally driven as a matter of principle.

Indeed, the resilience of many of the more developed countries, including our own, owes much to a broad-based educational approach that has placed a significant value on educating
the mind so that its products will be capable of contributing to
society across a range of issues and will have a framework for
later specialisation.

ENVIRONMENT

Apart from education, the other big 'E' is the environment, and
here there will be significant pressure to ensure more stringent
standards worldwide. The signs are already there and it is clear
that the major manufacturers are already taking their responsibilities very seriously.

Environmentally-friendly technologies are therefore likely to
be increasingly 'built-in'. This issue is going to be a major one in
the next century and the state of preparedness in a number of

environmentally-sensitive industries in Ireland – particularly in chemicals – holds out the prospect of competitive advantage.

TRANSPARENCY

As we approach the new millennium we live in a world of increasing transparency. It is a social and political issue as well as a matter for industry and business. People will argue about the efficiency of this and it must be said that transparency can cause problems as well as advancing the well-being of society. On balance, however, it is to be welcomed and regardless of what position we take, it will continue to be a feature of life in the twenty-first century.

Increased transparency will require other virtues. As more information is made available, more pressure will be put on communications requirements. The business of communicating information is vastly under-rated as a skill. From the outside, everyone assumes that it is the simplest thing in the world. For anyone concerned with running a business the scene is very different. What to communicate and to whom? How should it be done? What circumstances alter normal operating arrangements? What about confidentiality? All these are bread-and-butter issues but they are issues that crop up constantly in business today and will do so to an even greater extent in the future under the pressure of transparency. Information increases exponentially; it breeds a demand for more. The more information that is shared, the greater the possibilities for involving employees in the businesses in which they are employed.

As expectations for information increase, the next century will bring an explosion of developments impossible to forecast. They will not be centrally driven. Rather they will reflect the more individualist approach to work already apparent. Also – and in apparent contradiction – they will emanate from the increasing trend towards team work as a means of accepting greater responsibility and job satisfaction.

LEADERSHIP

All of this new order will bring with it a range of challenges. Some of these are properly in the court of business, some in the area of public policy. If we take further progress in technology, innovation and research and development as given, in the context of the volumes of change which we anticipate, then the biggest challenges for business are those found in education, training and skills-development, communications, employee involvement, human resource management, and above all in leadership.

The next century has all the ingredients to make it an exceptional phase in the development of our planet. Challenges there are aplenty. There are also exciting possibilities. To maximise the potential for achievement will require courage and leadership from policy-makers. Just as competition is increasingly global, so is policy-making. There need not be a contradiction between ever-increasing competitive pressures and the solutions of some of our most intractable problems. Political action on a global scale will be necessary to deal with many of these, particularly the North/South divide. The shifts in industrial development, the revolution in services and distribution, the increased expectation of many in our society for ever-improving standards will not be easy to manage.

The prospects are so extraordinarily intriguing that one can only look forward with considerable excitement.

Bill Attley

The Future Is Not What It Used to Be

Bill Attley is general secretary of SIPTU, and a board member
of FÁS, the Irish Trade Board, NCIR (the National College of
Industrial Relations), the Irish Institute for European Affairs,
and RTE.

In considering the role of labour unions and the Left and their
potential contribution in creating the future it is essential to
debunk some of the historical myth and claims associated with
Thatcherism/Reaganism. Many have come to view the way in
which the world had changed, and is still changing, as somehow
synonymous with a new world order which Thatcherism/Reagan-
ism claimed to lead. Failure by the Left during the eighties to
identify the range and scale of changes underway provided the
political opportunity for these leaders of the Right to make such
claims successfully, at least for a while.

The reality is that Thatcher/Reagan had better advice on the
momentous changes underway worldwide than did the Left. The
old post-war arrangements were crumbling. The economic and
social systems of the Eastern bloc were collapsing. Fundamental
changes in technology and the nature of production of goods and
services were radically altering the manner and locations in
which work was now being done. Simultaneously, a new more
fragmented and variegated society and culture was emerging, globally. Thatcherism/Reaganism sought to appropriate this new world
order for itself, emphasising the market as supreme arbiter while
shaping the perceptions of the emerging order both through

policy and practice, and culturally, by promoting a new entrepreneurial culture. The Left failed to differentiate between such claims by Thatcher/Reagan and large-scale changes actually taking place in the world and is now faced with having to unravel this emergent post-industrial culture in order to provide the parameters for a new politics of the Left more in tune with the dilemmas and opportunities facing workers in today's radically changing world. In doing this the Left is forced into a real engagement with the new identities, and the new agendas, of the social and political groupings emerging. The challenge and opportunity this represents for renewal is as immense as it is profound, as the old visions and the orthodoxy which had nurtured them for almost a century have been undermined and overtaken by history.

There is reason for measured optimism in attempting this, however, as analysis shows that while Thatcherite society speaks a language of choice, freedom and autonomy, as a political entity it is a spent force, increasingly characterised by inequality, division and authoritarianism. The reality is that the scale of the changes in the new world emerging are more monumental and more profound than Thatcherism/Reaganism, which increasingly appears anachronistic, modernising on the one hand, while simultaneously introducing ever more repressive and regressive policies which are essentially backward-looking. The reality is that the guiding principles underlying the political leadership of the conservative Right are inadequate to the needs of people in the emerging world of the twenty-first century. People will not accept rising levels of homelessness, nor do they aspire to having jobs at less than subsistence levels of pay. These are political realities which will not be wished away – as witnessed by the virtual meltdown of the Conservative vote in the recent British by-elections.

NO PRE-DETERMINED ENDGAME

There is no implicit or inevitable destiny for any 'side' built into the new emerging order. The struggle between the social democratic forces of the Left and more reactionary and regressive forces will continue, although in different arenas and involving new and different issues. Other influential political and social groupings will emerge also with radically new agendas which will impact on the debate. Examples of this can be seen in the capacity of present-day women's groups, or indeed groups organised around issues such as animal rights or Green issues, to dominate or at least radically alter the agendas of both Left and Right. The outcome could indeed be a greater erosion of, rather than a deepening of, democracy and culture unless the Left successfully faces down the challenges inherent in the new order.

Emerging Strategic Thinking of the Left in Ireland

While the Left has been slow to move with the times, few in this country would successfully argue about its ability to catch up quickly and convincingly. Contrasting our experience in Ireland with that of Britain, or indeed the United States, clearly the trade union movement here learned from experiences elsewhere, adopting significantly different strategies to deal with the new realities.

The thinking underlying Irish labour unions' entry into, and continuing involvement with, a pluralist view of society and the management of the economy through the mechanism of Social Partnership is both pragmatic and strategic. Prior to the PNR (Programme for National Recovery), a decade of free collective bargaining produced a negative net result in the pockets of workers with unions exercising little significant influence over the economic and social decisions affecting their members. Despite the limitations of the current strategy, it has resulted in a stable economy with high growth rates, increased numbers of jobs (albeit not enough of them), and modest but real wage increases linked to increasing productivity over time and a continuing presence at national level with key elements of its agenda recognised and included in successive national agreements between the key Social Partners.

By adopting flexible attitudes to new management technologies and production systems, unions are encouraging employers and government to galvanise all economic effort behind a strategy to deal with the markets of the new international circumstance in a concerted manner in order to maximise the numbers of opportunities and jobs for workers in Ireland. Unions are committed to the further development of this view in the decades ahead. Coupled with this win/win approach is a sustained campaign to encourage government to change social and taxation regulations to match the changing nature of work, thus facilitating workers to participate in the world of work in all of its emerging variations without fear of unnecessary penalty for so doing.

To limit the trauma of unemployment and reduce the wide-scale uncertainty which an increasingly rapidly changing work scene involves, it is essential that mobile individual work-related rights be established. Thus, while jobs for life may indeed decline, individual workers will move from one job to another more easily, taking with them their various social, pension and other 'credits' necessary to sustain them during periods of under-employment or training, and in sickness and old age. The positive contribution this cross-fertilisation will bring to the development of all work and social organisations in Ireland should not be under-estimated. Clearly, the attitude of unions and employers will be critical in facilitating the emergence of such a flexible and mobile labour force based on appropriate support systems.

Conscious of the nature of the emerging information intensive knowledge-based economy, unions will be increasingly seeking an extension of the concept of continuing training and education.

It will gradually become the norm for workers to continue learning throughout their working lives. In the new circumstance there will be a greater blurring of the distinction between work and learning. Given the vital importance of learning and adaptation in the new order, it is likely that labour unions will themselves develop core competencies in accessing and delivery of such training and learning for their members. Clearly, here too there is the basis for joint initiatives involving both sides of industry.

GLOBALISATION OF PROBLEM-SOLVING MACHINERY

Problems associated with the emerging new circumstance transcend the nation state and will not be capable of being dealt with within national boundaries. The huge increase in the numbers, resources and agendas of international inter-governmental and non-governmental agencies and organisations developed during the past two decades is evidence of this trend. The Left, and particularly labour unions, will have to increasingly internationalise their activities in order to influence and regulate forces which would otherwise undermine their agendas and their constituency. Their successes in this area will be of interest to management also, as the establishment of universal standards in areas such as quality, safety, wages and specific work conditions will help ensure all enterprises are operating on a level playing field.

Thatcherism viewed the new emerging circumstance narrowly and solely in terms of markets. This overlooked the enormous scale of changes included; its inherent capacity to bring about the decay of the nation state, national cultures and identities; and the scale of the crises which would follow as the world re-orders itself socially and politically. Equally, it ignored the emerging larger crisis of the planet itself which will require an entirely new relationship between humans and the environment.

As the knowledge content of work and products expands, the

physical labour and raw materials requirement is continuously contracting. In today's global economy information is rapidly becoming the key raw material, the skills threshold of jobs is rising and the technological intensity of economic activity is increasing. The only way to meet the challenges resulting from these developments is to move forward, not backwards.

THE ENVIRONMENT – EMERGING CONCERNS

Unions will also be forced to embrace the wider view, some elements of which will be alien to their more traditional concerns. Environmental issues, for example, will increasingly dominate the lives of workers: issues relating to global warming; depletion of the ozone layer; the impact of harmful chemicals; the impact of burning fossil fuels; clean energy and clean production technologies; safe products and processes; the elimination of waste production; recycling; elimination of CO_2 and SO_2 emissions. Unions will join with other progressive forces in pursuing strategies to deal with problems arising in such areas. Part of the paradox of the new circumstance is that, while fewer people will be needed to manufacture all the products that are needed, emerging environmental crises and new pressure for higher standards will offer equally large-scale opportunities for new work and new jobs.

Ultimately, competition will pressure workers and employers in different parts of the world to identify and produce those goods and services which offer some unique competitive advantage. In this, environment is a critical factor, especially as increasingly stringent international standards and consumer demand will not permit trade in products which are contaminated by a wide range of materials which are already an integral part of many environments, eg, pesticides, nuclear contaminants, etc. It will be in Irish workers' interests to ensure our environment is protected to the highest possible levels to ensure our long-term capability to use it to underpin the quality of many of our products, including our vital agriculture, agri-manufacturing and tourist industries. For these, and other related reasons, unions of the future will be likely to support an increasingly Green agenda.

OLD FORMS OF COMPETITION REDUNDANT

Interdependence and cooperation are the hallmarks of a pluralist society and with emerging globalisation old forms of competition based on national or economic interests simply will not work. This is becoming increasingly obvious even within the European Union. The future is emerging out of the collapse of elements of the past. And just as nobody is actually 'in charge', the shape and nature of the future is up for grabs. The Left is faced with an unprecedented challenge to analyse the forces of change successfully and to create the necessary strategic alliances and policies to represent workers in a society which otherwise risks becoming even more fragmented and inequitable than heretofore.

Because unions in Ireland have the necessary experience of dealing with large numbers of people with diverse views, of large systems and of change, and also possess the necessary knowledge and organisation ability, they will continue to act as a major cohesive influence in an emerging future which is fraught with possibilities for conflict. Well before 2020, unions will have adjusted their structures in response to the particular needs of all sectors of the labour force and will continue to shape the social and economic agenda with other progressive forces in society. Having undergone such profound change themselves, they will also become a vital source of expertise for other like-minded groups both nationally and internationally. Employers based in Ireland will also adjust to the new emerging world order and in doing this will also be faced with a number of interesting choices regarding their intended relationship with labour unions.

MANAGEMENT OF CHANGE INVOLVES
MANAGEMENT ITSELF CHANGING

Those managements who have not already opted to include their own workforce in a real partnership in managing enterprises will be forced to do so, sooner rather than later. The main reason will be competition with companies elsewhere which rely on the collective intelligence of their entire workforces as the key factor to ensuring success. A more educated population with radically different expectations of work will help bring this about more quickly. Teamwork will be the norm within the enterprise of the future, which will be epitomised by mutual respect and high levels of trust. Equally, employers cannot expect the continuation of a one-sided arrangement whereby they may organise themselves in whatever fashion, while workers should indefinitely tolerate refusal on their part to recognise unions as their chosen means for independent representation in the workplace. Increasing interdependence between the Social Partners reflects a world-wide phenomenon, and the example of Britain and the US, where workers' rights and entitlements to social supports are being destroyed wholesale, is not an ethical or appropriate model for managing the human resource of the advanced world economy that the future implies.

Mutual respect begins with recognition. Unions will not be waiting until 2020 to establish workers' rights in this regard. A positive shift in employer attitudes could speed up the process and I am hopeful that progress on meaningful participation and appropriate structures, which encourage everybody in an enterprise to bring their intelligence to bear on the issues and problems facing enterprises, will be introduced comprehensively a long time in advance of that.

Unions reject the idea that to create jobs, standards have to be sacrificed and regard strategies based on such notions as morally wrong, socially unjust in their likely impact, and economically outdated. The challenge instead is to strike a balance between individual freedom and social support. The task of unions is to renew themselves and consolidate in order that they will be able to provide the necessary impetus to ensure social cohesion and economic success in the future.

WE CAN SOLVE THE ISSUE OF UNEMPLOYMENT

The idea that it is appropriate, or just, or humane, or that it is sustainable for a small island economy to exclude some 20% of its population from meaningful involvement in the workplace is an abomination. Apart from that, it is a tragic waste of our most valuable resource – intelligence. While some measures are being attempted to reduce the levels of unemployment, and new options developed which focus particularly on the long-term unemployed, we actually have to resolve this issue. Setting a target date for doing so by 2020 might be a very worthwhile and workable idea. Numbers of countries around the world have consistently maintained high employment levels, ensuring that not more then 5% of their working population are out of work at any time. I do not believe it beyond our collective imaginations to analyse how this was achieved and to do likewise. In the meantime the creation of a national minimum income is a key priority.

Our present institutionalised helplessness is beneath contempt. The psychological violence done to people excluded in this way comes back to roost as we face into spiralling levels of crime, substance abuse, violence both within the family and elsewhere and the increasing costs of associated medical care and incarceration. There must be a better way. Unions have traditionally been a singular but consistent voice in pursuing a reasonable deal for the unemployed. It is a mistaken view that wages can be depressed by maintaining high levels of unemployed or that a low pay economy would increase the number of jobs all round. Third World countries abound where exploitation of this kind is now the norm. Ireland could not compete with the levels of 'pay' involved in maintaining such 'jobs'. The reality is that the world economy of 2020 will be knowledge intensive and will sustain relatively high pay levels throughout the developed world. We must be part of that scenario. Anything else would be disastrous both for our industrial capability and, ultimately, our people.

ELIMINATING OTHER FORMS OF EXCLUSION

Work restructuring brings with it new possibilities for more thoughtful organisation and scheduling which will facilitate women, single parents, and those with disabilities or limited skills or limited work experience, to participate in the workplace. Employers and unions will need to look more creatively at ways in which this can be achieved. And there is no need for this to give rise to increased costs. It is an attitude issue, not unlike some assumptions underlying much industrial software on the market at the moment which automatically assumes that systems developed for the workplace must necessarily be about control of the labour element. Imaginative programming elsewhere has brought about shifts in the direction of inclusion, responsibility, and self regulation which have proved themselves to be far more successful change-management strategies. Because it is more cost effective and socially desirable, companies which operate socially supportive and people-friendly work systems in the future will be provided with special tax credits to ensure they remain competitive.

Companies in 2020 will, by and large, no longer be owned by small numbers of individuals. Instead they will be 'owned' and managed by groupings of stakeholders. These will include worker representatives, and representatives of the societies they operate in and on which they depend for a myriad of supports. They will increasingly operate as a member of the community in which they function – and all that entails. Unions, no less so.

Gradually, with the globalisation of production, the decline of the nation state, the rise of the individual, the Greening of politics and the increasing speed with which new products become redundant, new pressures will emerge, forcing us to alter our relationship with the environment and to rediscover community and the unique value of personal relationships. The seeds of such developments are already evident all around us. Organisations, once a defence against anxiety rather than a response to human needs, will increasingly fall away, giving way to networks of relationship which are more immediately and profoundly supportive. Ethically-based, open systems, they will be responsive and yet cease to exist beyond the resolution of the problems which prompted their creation. People will behave in a similar fashion and the current paranoia about the future will give way to a more intuitive and pragmatic attitude which will itself fuel appropriate invention and entertainment.

Future exchanges will increasingly involve higher levels of trust based on an implicit assumption that each party will provide whatever goods or services to the best of their actual ability. Because we must choose friendship or cease to exist we will operate open systems which make it abundantly clear where the truth lies. In short, that trust is about to become verifiable at every stage and at every level. Current individual and organisation strategies, based on greed and primitive forms of competition, ignore the greater and longer-term value of firmly based cooperative strategies. There is increasing public demand for higher standards and not just as they apply to goods and services. Business, political parties and all large organisations are increasingly required to operate to the highest ethical standards. Transparency, accountability and freedom of information will ensure that those who transgress will be eliminated from the marketplace.

We are either going to learn to live together peacefully, in relative harmony with one another and our environment, or we will cease to exist. This will require a major shift in our thinking and behaviour, far surpassing any technological change or advance we have witnessed to date or are likely to in the future. Fortunately, there are forces at work which will help make this possible.

Matthew Dempsey

Outlook for Agriculture

Matthew Dempsey is editor and chief executive officer of
the *Irish Farmers Journal*, former chairman of the Agricultural Institute and ACOT.

Twenty-five years ago membership of the European Union for
Ireland was an unattained aspiration. Twenty-five years from
now, there will, in all probability, be twenty-three full-time
members of the European Union (EU).

We under-estimate the technical and demographic revolution
that has taken place in Irish agriculture over the last twenty-five
years. This technical revolution has accompanied a dramatic
reduction in the real price of food.

World growth in agricultural output is continuing to slacken.
Global agricultural production grew by 3% per annum in the
1960s, by 2.4% in the 1970s, and by 2.2% in the 1980s. The
Food and Agricultural Organisation of the United Nations (FOA)
has forecast this figure to drop to 1.8% over the next twenty
years. Already in the 1990s, pressure points in world food
supplies are appearing. For the first time, China has been
unable to supply North Korea with grain. The United States has
stepped in to fill the breach. All set-aside has been scrapped in
the US.

In retrospect, will the mid-nineties be seen as a temporary blip,
or for the next twenty-five years are we, in fact, seeing the
Malthusian nightmare begin to come to reality?

At least part of the key to the formation of our vision for the year 2020 lies in the Far East – especially China.

World population by the year 2020 is forecast to reach 8.3 billion, compared with a little over five billion today. But the significant growth in that population is not going to take place in Western Europe – or in Ireland.

The basic constituents of Irish agricultural output have changed, but not dramatically, over the last two hundred years. The grass base that has underpinned Irish agriculture since Brehon times will still apply. Some land will move in or out of grain, depending on relative price relationships, but it looks as if the phenomenal transformation that has taken place in Irish grain, especially winter wheat, will not be repeated over the next twenty-five years (see Table I).

Table I / Yield of Common Wheat – 100 kg/HA

	1973	1990
France	45.7	66.1
United Kingdom	40.4	69.1
Ireland	39.1	82.1

The great beverage industries of Ireland – beer and spirits – will still need major supplies of malting barley, but the great imponderable is how the relative prices of grain and beef will develop. The trend since 1914 (see Table II) has been an inexorable fall in the relative price of grain, ensuring that greater amounts would be used. At the same time, the conversion efficiency of the pig and poultry industries has improved dramatically. As people become richer, they eat more meat; this is expected to happen explosively in China and India over the next twenty years. The effects will be felt in Ireland in two ways:

  ▶ a rise in the real price of grain;
  ▶ a steadily increasing demand for beef.

Table II – Relative Prices (current prices)

	Consumer Price Index	Wheat/ton	Bullocks Fat>3yrs per head	Milk per gallon	Min average wages per week
1914	100	£ 8.75	£16.9	2.02p	–
1924	188	£13.00	£23.2	3.78p	£ 1.3
1992	5913	£110.00	£680.0*	100p	£127.24

* over 550kg

While we are at this stage (in mid-1995) relatively near to the world price of grain, but far below it for beef, Ireland's total ruminant population (the sum of dairy cows, beef cattle and sheep) is at its highest ever level.

The essential questions that have to be answered concerning the policy framework up to the year 2020 are:

- will the Common Agricultural Policy (CAP) still be in existence with common financing as a core value?
- will the European legislative framework be more or less environmentally rigorous than at present?
- will the national governments have a commitment – backed up by cash – to maintaining a rural population throughout the nation states?

In straight cost of production terms, Irish farmers can compete with anyone in Europe but not, in the case of sheep meat or dairy products, with New Zealand, nor, in the case of wheat or beef, with Argentina (see Table III). To be competitive does not imply being the lowest cost producer in the world but rather being one who can sell his product at a lower price than that of the weakest competitor remaining in the market.

On that basis Irish agriculture in the year 2020 will be producing beef, dairy products, grain crops. The greatest potential difference lies not in the make-up of the output, even though mushrooms, nursery stock and new enterprises such as deer and forestry will probably have expanded by then; the major differ-ence is likely to be in the make-up of the farming population.

Table III – The Competitive Advantage of Irish Agriculture / 1989 costs, £ per 100 kg

	MILK	CEREALS	LIVEWEIGHT LAMB
France	12.6	6.7	122.7
Denmark	19.9	12.6	–
Ireland	11.3	7.1	84.1
UK	13.2	10.2	89.6
US	17.8	7.8	–
New Zealand	5.2/7.8	–	40

Source: *Irish Farmers Journal*/AIB study by Dr G Boyle, Maynooth University

The percentage of household farm income accounted for by non-farm income has been growing consistently and steadily. The removal of the marriage bar in the banks and a decentral-ised civil service has had an enormous influence on the stabil-ity and development of family farming on what would be considered non-viable farms throughout the country. This is an international trend. While it has not stopped an intensification in land use it has certainly curtailed an intensification in land ownership.

The number of those engaged in full-time farming has been and is declining continuously and can be expected to continue to decline by 4-5% a year – based on that trend we can expect to see no more than 40,000 to 50,000 people engaged in full-time farming in Ireland by the year 2020 (see Table IV). However, it should be noted that the number of those with land but devoting between zero and half of their time to farming has stayed remark-ably static over the last twenty years at around 160,000. In another twenty-five years it seems that, unless there are dramatic changes in policy, this group will continue to number around 120,000 to 150,000.

Table IV – Dairy Farmer Numbers

1985	77,000
1987	69,000
1989	57,000
1991	45,000

From this juncture, the year 2020 seems far away, but assessed over the developmental period of a sector such as agriculture, it is only part of a continuum. The sixties in Ireland were in many ways a decade of anticipation. In the seventies, the anticipation turned into reality and output boomed. In the eighties constraints on production began to reappear. The nineties sees environmental considerations take on a new focus.

The first decade of the new century will be dominated by the absorption of the Eastern and Central European states into the European Union. The political imperative will be to have as little change as possible in the agricultural framework affecting the existing member states. In the years up to 2010 approximately we can expect to see a new GATT round which will nudge us closer to a type of world free trade in agricultural goods. But, Europe will not be ready to accept the intense regional specialisation which this, pushed to its logical conclusion, would bring. We will have modifications to the status quo, but the status quo will be recognisable. We will almost certainly see a scaling down in the grants payable for afforestation. The hand-wringing over the payment of large individual sums to specialist grain growers in East Anglia and the Paris Basin will probably have resulted in some kind of ceiling on payments per farm or per person employed per farm. In dairying, after much huffing and puffing, we will probably still have an element of the quota regime, but it may well be mixed with a lower support price and a premium payment per cow, with a ceiling of somewhere around 60 to 80 cows per farmer. In the sheepmeat sector, production will be tilted even more decisively to the disadvantaged areas. The political concessions made to New Zealand in the 1994 GATT round, which gave them unlimited access in the form of chilled vac-pac cuts, will have to be extended to those in Eastern Europe. Ireland is unlikely to be able to fight totally by itself on the sheep front. Disadvantaged area producers can look forward to increasing rural world premium top-ups, but with a continuing limitation on the volume of output fully supported.

On beef, the great imponderable is the consumption level within Europe. We have seen a catastrophic long-term decline in the real price and in the actual consumption of wool. We face the same in beef, unless the consumer health reservations are resolutely tackled. The future for Irish beef production, because of the low cost of weight gained while the animals are on grass, is assured. What is not assured is the place of an Irish beef industry dependent on supplies of imported grain at above EU mainland prices. By the year 2010 we can expect to see Irish beef going to North Africa in a bulk commodity type framework and specialised high-value cuts beginning to make an impact in Japan, Korea and perhaps China. There is no reason to expect that the historical low return on capital invested in beef will change. With the inevitable emphasis on part-time farming by many service and industrial workers, low intensity, small-scale beef production will remain a feature of the Irish rural landscape. For those firms serious about supplying a still rich continental Europe with high quality steer beef, Irish agribusiness will, by the year 2020, have established a network of supply depots and infrastructural facilities across Europe. These firms will be contracting with Irish farmers for the supply of a standard beef product all the year round.

While the changes within the farm gate will be gradual but significant over the next twenty-five years, the changes in the processing industry are likely to be explosive.

A number of key food companies, private, co-op and plc, are now of international scale. The typical Irish agribusiness manager has shown a capacity to span the cultural differences from Japan to the United States. Twenty-five years ago, aiming to have a number of companies with turnover in excess of a billion pounds seemed an outlandish aspiration. By the year 2020, on the present rates of growth, there will be Irish organisations with Irish-owned sophisticated production and distribution facilities for the core dairy and meat products right across Europe and beyond. For a small country, we make an impact far beyond what the scale of our population would suggest. We under-estimate the cultural change that has occurred in our educational system and which is preparing the next generation of Irish people to take their place in the business sun.

To sum up. For the majority, the future in Irish farming will continue to depend on conventional farming, coupled with some form of ancillary income. For most, this ancillary income will be by way of wage or salary earned off farm. A few will diversify into tourism or specialist ventures, but these will be in the minority and where successful they will develop into thriving local industries. But diversification is not an easy road and calls for special attributes of energy, entrepreneurial skill and knowledge. The very intensive sectors of poultry and pigs have moved away, to a large extent, from being farmer-dominated businesses. This trend is likely to intensify, with the farmyards being no more than production sites for the major food processing and feed compounding firms.

Irish agriculture will continue to be predominantly grass based. The technological break-throughs that have placed the tillage sector on a new plateau of productivity have been achieved, but no great expansion can be expected over the next two and a half decades. Successful farmers, because of per capita payment limitations, will tend to invest outside of agriculture, which will curtail the developments that an unfettered free market would let loose. The pivotal change that occurred in 1973, which gave free access to EU markets, will still be the predominant force.

Patrick O'Neill

The Death of Supply-Side Management

Patrick O'Neill is group managing director of Avonmore Foods plc, director of Forbairt, the Irish Permanent Building Society, the Irish Co-op Petroleum and Norish (Kilkenny) Ltd.

It is a significant challenge to compose a vision of what business in Ireland will be like twenty-five years hence. A useful personal target might be to live long enough to review the predictions.

One way of endeavouring to provide some scoping for the exercise is to review the developments in Ireland since 1970. I wonder what we would have said twenty-five years ago about the shape of Ireland in 1995? We certainly would not have anticipated having 300,000 people unemployed, or using desk-top computers on a daily basis. Neither would we have predicted that the emerging co-ops of the late sixties and early seventies would grow into food companies with a turnover in excess of £1 billion per annum and operations on several continents.

As I write this article the most dramatic developments which are occurring that are likely to impact on all citizens over the next twenty-five years are in the areas of information and communications technologies. These technologies will make possible products and services which were only a dream a few years ago. The interaction of television and information systems has enormous potential for business and individuals in their private lives. The experts are already predicting a 500-channel television cable and we will be significantly impacted by the degree to which we embrace these new resources.

As chief executive of a food company I have an abiding interest in consumers. As society changes with smaller families and greater access to travel and information, the challenge for food companies to respond to the evolving preferences of our customers is demanding. Early in the next century more than 50% of food consumed in the developed world will be prepared (if not consumed) outside the home. The developments in this direction have already facilitated the growth of multinational catering establishments such as McDonald's, Burger King, Wendy's, Pizza Hut, Dominos Pizza, to name but a few. These superb participants in the food chain are providing an identifiable diet for consumers on every continent. This is leading to the globalisation of our customer base and potentially creating an international market for high quality food produced to exacting specifications, but priced very competitively. I believe this trend will accelerate over the next twenty-five years and that family meals at home will account for no more than five 'eating opportunities' per week.

The vast supply of data and its ease of access will bear down relentlessly on the operating costs of every business – whether that is an individual farmer-producer or someone involved in processing, marketing or distribution. It is now reasonably well-established that increased scale leads to greater efficiency and lower costs. In the past this has been achieved in state enterprises through the introduction of national monopolies in the energy, transport and telecommunications sectors. The dis-establishment of these monopolies over the next ten years will create a need for scale to be achieved through international alliances. In the food industry we are a long way from monopolistic structures and, in fact, the disparate nature of the sector will not sustain in the competitive world of the twenty-first century. We will do well to put together two or three world-class multinational food companies with sales in excess of £5 billion each within the next ten years and the target of having these companies reach the £10 billion turnover level in the subsequent decade. It will be a major challenge for the Irish producer base to respond to these developments and, ideally, maintain a substantial degree of influence through the shareholding in these Irish food multinationals.

The producer base will probably decline significantly in the early part of the next century and it is possible that we will have no more than one-quarter of our present farmers actively engaged on the land by the year 2020. This will have social and economic implications for rural Ireland and the major towns in the provinces. It will be important that governments take on board the future shape of Irish agriculture and provide the necessary leadership to all who are interested in the sector in order to ensure that the way forward is planned to optimise the impact which such radical change will inevitably have. Recent speeches by the Taoiseach and Minister for Agriculture, Food and Forestry, provide some encouragement that a longer term perspective is being addressed and that the Ireland of free trade and an Exchequer shorn of structural funds will still prosper.

As producers and the food industry internationally adapt to inevitable changes in diet, information and technology, we will also have to accommodate more regulation and the impact of pressure groups. The World Trade Organisation (WTO) will move forward to liberalise trade further and in so doing will generate further regulations to ensure that artificial barriers are frustrated. Concurrent with this development there is deregulation at the operating company level with employees increasingly paid on output and, in the United States, an infinitely more flexible approach to mobility. There is a real danger that within the European Union we will have four or five tiers of regulations, whereas the United States and the emerging countries of the Pacific Rim will only be governed by WTO conditions. Our ability to compete could be seriously jeopardised in such circumstances and it may well be that over the next ten years the European Union will be at a serious competitive disadvantage because of labour regulations, environmental restrictions, packaging requirements and a host of other dictates. While the Chinese and others drive forward uninhibited by any vast bureaucracy we may, therefore, suffer a market share decline. Eventually we will start unwinding the panoply of laws and statutory instruments so that we can free up the energies of Europeans to compete internationally.

One of the questions which stimulates much discussion and disagreement at the present time is who will produce the food of the future. On the one hand we have China with 22% of the world's population, but only 7% of the arable land. At the same time there are greatly under-utilised agricultural resources in Africa, South America and Eastern Europe.

Furthermore, we have the economically illogical supply-side management of food production in the European Union, the net effects of which are to frustrate the advances of technology at farm level, which have an enormous capacity to increase agricultural output, and, on the other hand, to surrender growing markets to countries such as Australia, the United States and New Zealand. These countries have the common sense to allow the laws of supply and demand to govern output. The one prediction I would make with some certainty about the next twenty-five years is that the bureaucratic love-child of supply-side management will expire. The last great attempt by producers to rip off consumers through restricted output was by OPEC. With oil prices having peaked at $34 per barrel it is a measure of the oil cartel's failure that supplies are now readily available at less than $20 per barrel. The tyranny of production cartels is usually defeated by the emergence of alternative sources of supply (non-OPEC countries had a major impact on destroying that cartel's power) or the development of substitutes. The artificially high food prices in

Europe, which are underpinned by the intervention system, have generated the development of dairy spreads in the milk sector and greatly increased poultry consumption in the meat sector. Inevitably, economic forces always win and unless we can produce food economically our markets will be forfeited to lower cost producers or acceptable substitutes.

One of the great deficiencies in Irish society is the low level of esteem in which entrepreneurs are held. The education system has not placed an adequate emphasis on entrepreneurship and this has led to an entirely inadequate level of business start-ups in Ireland compared to other European countries and, in particular, the United States. Fortunately, greater access to travel and modern communications are making it more difficult for 'the powers that be' to restrict the curiosity and genius of young Irish people to the classics, the law and other worthy, if unproductive, activities. I believe we will see in the next quarter century a great flowering of small business developments which will provide the motive power for the large and powerful companies of the mid-century. This process would be greatly stimulated by real tax breaks for young people who start their own business while ensuring that those who entered the comfort arena of 'permanent and pensionable' would pay more punitive tax rates.

Roy Baille

Tomorrow, the World

Roy Bailie is chairman of the W & G Baird group of companies, member of the Northern Irish Tourist Board, and the Industrial Development Board (IDB).

Shortly after World War II, the man who founded the IBM empire said 'the world couldn't possibly need more than five computers'. This proves two things: the bigger the mistake, the greater the learning opportunity; and that the rolling advances in technology can only be plotted or predicted a few years ahead, if at all. (Apparently, the next change in information technology – IT – is going to be literally a quantum change: computers based on quantum physics which will be able to perform almost limitless parallel calculations, thus increasing speed and capacity to unimaginable levels.)

Technology is one aspect of change that is of central concern to my business – printing and publishing; the other is the environment. Both of these will be crucial to Irish business in general during the early years of the next century.

THE EUROPEAN UNION'S 'NORTHERN ARC'

What will business in Ireland be like in twenty-five years' time? I suspect that the question posed by the Royal Dublin Society (RDS) should be rewarded by replacing 'Ireland' with 'Europe' – and even, possibly, 'the world'. With the European Free Trade Association (EFTA) and the European Union (EU) together forming the

European Economic Area, a multinational market-place of nineteen nations and four hundred million consumers, and the effects of the GATT agreement being realised, the world is set to become a global village not just in terms of communications, but also as a market-place. This will have profound implications for business in Ireland which traditionally looked to its immediate neighbour or to the East as a core market. Paradoxically, markets in mainland Europe have seemed more remote than traditional markets in Canada and the US. In a recent article J G Martin, Head of Commission of the Amalgamated Engineering Union (AEU) in the UK, drew attention to the Northern Arc, a body seeking to represent northern regional interests in an ever-expanding Europe. Sharing common problems of peripherality, geographical or political trade barriers and poor East-West transport infrastructure, the Arc stretches from Ireland, across Northern England and Scotland, Denmark, the Baltic, Poland and North Germany. Pilot projects are already planned, covering transportation, shipping services, regional freight movement, trade development and new forms of cultural and ecological tourism. The focus will be on telecommunications.

Technology. Geography. Environment. Business in Ireland must reconcile these three factors, using the first in a way that will minimise the economic disadvantages of the second, and maintain the environmental and ecological richness that is steadily becoming perceived as one of the island's key competitive advantages. In a world that is becoming smaller and more competitive, we have to forge new links, not only in marketing but in identifying common problems and solutions and forming economic alliances.

THE INFORMATION REVOLUTION

My business is as subject to the effects of change as any other. It is an important sector for Irish business and one which, with modern communications, is potentially less disadvantaged by geography than heavier manufacturing – and, thus, a sector which can be steadily expanded. The printing, publishing and information industry in this island can grow substantially – but we have to stay alert to technological change.

We are currently living through what is being called the Third Revolution. The *first* was the Urban Revolution, when man, the hunter-gatherer, discovered that crops could be grown and animals domesticated, and began to settle in one place. The *second* was, of course, the Industrial Revolution which was ignited only 150 years ago, when steam power was first harnessed.

The *third* revolution is the Information Revolution, which began with the electronic computer. Its progress, as we all know, has been mind-boggling. The one constant is that it's virtually impossible to see what's round the next research and development (R&D) corner (though we do know that it's likely to be out of date in five years). Those who do not stay alert to change – particularly in our business – risk the fate of the dinosaurs.

Jacques Santer, the president of the European Commission, recently said: 'The development of the information society must be truly global, open to all and benefitting everyone. The dawn of the new age is upon us; it is not intergalactic pipedreams nor futurists running wild.'

We are in 'the information society', like it or not, and the printer's stock in trade – apart from ink and paper – is information. Where will our industry be in another hundred years? Where will business be, in general? We need to take that wider view because our industry is essentially a supply industry, whether to publishers, marketeers, government or manufacturers.

Again, the two main challenges to Irish and global business are clear. The first is environmental: how do we achieve continuing economic growth while sustaining our environment, from a global level right down to the discharge from our own sewers? The second is technological: will the pace and nature of technological change make us redundant in every sense of the word?

The legacy of both the first and second revolution has had negative aspects as well as positive ones arising from economic growth. Environmental pollution and social imbalances are two. Will the information society manage to avoid or even overcome the worst excesses of urban and industrial society? And what part can we play as printers?

THE PACE OF CHANGE

The pace of change is a third challenge to business. It is only within the past hundred years that Marconi was granted the first patent of a system of communication by means of electromagnetic waves (1896); that Wilbur Wright patented his aeroplane (1906); and that the first regular airmail service across the Atlantic began (1939), using flying boats from New York to Lisbon and Marseilles. Now we have faxes, largely making these three advances redundant, at least for the transmission of information.

Our industry, printing, is unrecognisable from the one I entered as a compositor in the 1960s. In this century alone we have seen vast changes in printing processes. Hand typesetting changed to linotype just a hundred years ago – and this technology persisted, in W & G Baird at least, until 1978 when it was replaced by the phototypesetting process and the expansion of lithography.

The acceleration in the pace of technology change during the past twenty years is well-reflected in printing with word-processing, computerised typesetting and laser printing, and the information revolution is now taking us beyond the printed word to multimedia and CD Rom, cable and interactive videos.

Printing has seen many threats come and go during this period, with Ceefax and Prestel, and computers: each supposed to augur the 'paperless office'. Yet, as we know all too well (those of us who make a tidy income from printing computer manuals), computer manufacturers are among the biggest producers of printed paper.

News of our death has been exaggerated, in other words, and I am not going to forecast that in the next century multimedia or CD Rom will carry death notices for the printed word. But there is one significant difference between these technologies and the previous harbingers of our doom. They still used the printed word as the medium of communication; most computers still do.

The new technologies, for the first time, provide the viewer with direct access to visual images and the spoken word; and not only with access, for images and words can be commanded, controlled and interacted with. Composers can transmit music, not just notes on paper; artists can transmit pictures, not just ideas in words; above all, educators can provide children with something very close to real experience without the effort of decoding print and harnessing imagination – virtual reality indeed.

Threat *or* opportunity?

In many ways, multimedia is a logical next step for our industry. If we don't take it, we're leaving the field open to the computer industry.

MULTIMEDIA

Multimedia is a much hyped but actually simple concept, made mysterious and esoteric by those with a vested interest in having it so. It simply means using a lot of different ways of presenting information.

If a company sends a letter out to someone outlining the services it can provide, it is using one medium to communicate. If they send a glossy brochure with colour photographs, they are using two media. If they also send a video with, say, Irish music on the sound track to create an atmosphere, that's a multimedia package. All the elements combine to give a better understanding of the messages being communicated.

Text, pictures, moving images (animation or picture) and sound; these elements are all familiar to us. Put them together with interactivity and it's a different matter again. The client receiving this package can choose what pieces of equipment, what corner of your factory, what sample of your work he or she wants to take a closer look at, ask questions about and so on.

Anybody with an Apple Mac already has access to DIY animation; to DIY video recording, editing and special effects; to DIY graphics and to incorporating their own photographs through a photo CD; to digital sound recording and editing; and to scanning, importing, copying and editing text from an external source like a newspaper or book and putting it together with graphics or video images.

If an enthusiast with an Apple Mac can create multimedia, it seems to me we should be doing it, too – especially bearing in mind that the falling price of successful, popular technology makes it affordable to a wide number of people very quickly.

Furthermore, one CD Rom disc can store the same quantity of computer data as four hundred floppy disks and contain over two hundred applications. This year 50% of the software from leading producers will be available on CD Rom rather than floppy disk. And when the technology becomes hand-held – then, what price books?

GLOBALISATION OF INFORMATION

On a wider front, the world of communications is shrinking more and more. The G7 summit in Brussels in February 1995 committed the world to a global information infrastructure, through projects including:

- cross-cultural education and training global networks to promote new ways of learning languages;

- electronic reference libraries, museums and galleries globally accessed via multimedia;
- global healthcare applications using networks and database to fight major diseases such as cancer and heart disease;
- small and medium enterprises: the development of networks to help businesses to find markets;
- and a global multimedia inventory of major projects which will promote the information society.

This is not new, just bigger and financially muscled up. Already, for example, for the price of a telephone call you can gain access to £12 billion-worth of EU-funded R&D: a goldmine of information, research and business opportunities, available free through the CORDIS programme.

Globalisation of information is the way things are inexorably going. If information really is our stock-in-trade, we have to think globally.

The Internet recently seems to have emerged out of the ether. But it already has almost forty million users, worldwide.

What is the Internet? What can it do? Where – if anywhere – is it going to take us? And what has it got to offer those of us in business, especially the communications business? If you agree that we have to think globally, then we have to think about the Internet.

THE INTERNET

In essence, it is a global web of interconnected computer networks. It was originally an open communications channel for US universities and research labs, set up in the 1960s by the Department of Defence. Now there are five million computers linked to the Internet, with around forty million users.

The Internet is fast changing from a research resource to a business forum: commercial users increased by 130% last year.

It is getting to the point that any business that needs to look beyond its own parish cannot afford to ignore what has become a global market-place. Whether we want access to information, worldwide data communications or to an electronic show window (there is a number of 'electronic malls' and 'shopping catalogues' in the Internet), then we should be looking at this as an opportunity.

Electronic mail is the main service provided by the Net and by far its most common use. Other services are:

- ▶ a news 'channel';
- ▶ advertising to relevant groups on bulletin boards;
- ▶ downloading software from one remote computer to another (though this is still specialist and non-commercial);
- ▶ conferences and discussion groups;
- ▶ libraries and databases with search facilities; many companies hold product information on it;
- ▶ sending CVs;
- ▶ electronic publishing – several newspapers have a daily presence on the Net, with news digests.

Many of the uses I mentioned earlier are directly relevant to what we as printers do, and given the sheer pace of technological development we are now used to, it is likely to be a central feature of commercial life within five or ten years.

Most commercial users of the Internet use the World Wide Web or 3W to present and retrieve information. 3W traffic increased by 350,000% last year. And – yes – the World Wide Web has multimedia capabilities, making it possible to present goods and services to millions of Web travellers who can read and view information and even place orders electronically. Everything from software and music to sex can be experienced – and bought – through the Web's multimedia capabilities. Magazines and newspapers from the *Irish Times* to *Playboy* are published on the Internet. Specialist 3W advertisement agencies have set up in the US; their art – given that a user can simply click to the next page if he or she gets bored – is to present persuasive information beneath a superstructure of fact and entertainment. (A new word – 'informercial' – has been coined, needless to say.) Record companies offer samples of new releases on video.

Now 1.1 million educational computer networks are linked to the Internet; and 1.3 million *commercial* computers with multiple users. If we are a service industry this is neither a market nor an area of technology that we can afford to neglect.

Put that argument together with the World Wide Web's multimedia capabilities – formatted text, sound, pictures, video and data transfer can be handled – and I think it's going to be better for us to be on the inside, looking out, rather that the other way round.

THE ENVIRONMENT – THREAT AND OPPORTUNITY

The other area of challenge for our industry, which I mentioned at the outset of this tentative foray into the future, is the environment. This also is an area which is increasingly global in its focus. We already have stringent European directives on industrial air pollution, waste management, water management and litter. We have the Montreal Protocol on phasing out chemicals which are believed to be damaging to the ozone layer. There is little doubt that the level of stringency will steadily increase during the next century, as we seek to create a sustainable future for the globe, and to overcome the worst environmental by-products of the first two global economic revolutions.

As the next century wears on, it is inevitable that companies which do not embrace and promote Green imperatives will run the risk of losing their competitive edge in a market-place where customers and, increasingly, the law, expect environmental concern and openness. The risk will increase to environmentally insensitive companies that funding, whether from financial institutions or private investment, will be dependent on good environmental performances. Poor environmental performers will find it increasingly difficult to attract employees, especially the bright, aware and committed young (and don't forget that one of the biggest environmental challenges facing developed economies in the next century is a falling birthrate and ageing population; we will need every advantage we can get, to attract the brightest and best people into industry).

Technology and the environment provide for Ireland, I believe, more in the way of opportunity than threat. The technological opportunities promise sustainable growth by minimising the effects of our peripheral geography and by offering minimal threat to the environment. The environmental opportunities arise from the richness of our landscape and ecology – and of our cultural and social diversity – in a world that is increasingly seeking escape from the effects of the Second Revolution.

Finbar Callan

With All the Hopes of Future Years

Finbar Callanan is director general of The Institution of
Engineers of Ireland

Recent history has demonstrated how difficult it is to forecast the
future. How many, just a few years ago, could have foreseen the
disappearance of the Berlin Wall, the conflict in Yugoslavia or
the collapse of the Soviet Union? Indeed, few could have foreseen
the accelerating process which led to the peace process in
Northern Ireland from a time when it appeared that little progress
was being made.

The future may be planned, and planning has contributed
significantly to the development of the Irish economy. However,
planning can be inhibited by the exigencies of party politics
which means that the vision of governments rarely extends beyond the four years' life of such administrations. What is needed
is a vision for Ireland by the people of Ireland which those who
are elected must implement and which sets out for all governments the desirable goals to be attained. Our early governments
and individual politicians had such visions which they pursued.
The fact that their visions were not often realised is not a reflection
on those who sought to look ahead, but rather a result of subsequent events and economic facts of life which inhibited much
of the development which the founding fathers of our state had
in mind.

The planning of the fifties and early sixties certainly left their mark on the Irish economy, but that was in an era when Ireland still had significant elements of the philosophy of *sinn féin* and a belief that 'ourselves alone' could bring prosperity to Ireland.

That vision, cloudy and green as it may have been, became cloudier as the decades moved on and growing international pressure and a dependency culture, created by reliance on foreign industry and on the European hand-out, blunted that earlier resolve to do it ourselves. Whatever advantages may have accrued to the country in recent decades by virtue of this new culture, we must recognise that in the new millennium, hand-outs may become less supportive and multinational business, which has little corporate conscience in this regard, will always relocate where the most favourable conditions exist.

In recent decades Ireland, with its European backing and the influence of multinational companies, has muddled forward, much as Britain, under the umbrella of North Sea oil, has ploughed a mediocre furrow. That will not be sufficient for the future and during the next twenty-five years, Ireland, in particular, has to work to a new vision and work hard at achieving it. In viewing Ireland, therefore, in the year 2020 we can approach it by expressing the hope that there will be a realisable vision which will be achieved.

THE SUPERHIGHWAY

Over-riding every consideration of our future is the impact of the Information Superhighway on future development, education, business, management, politics and culture. It is impossible to predict what the highway will produce and its effect on how we think and order our lives is yet to be assessed. It will be an era of potentially great opportunity and great threat, and the ingenuity of man, which will produce the new developments within the highway, will need to be matched by an equal ingenuity in protecting populations, their privacy, independence, individuality, process of thought and their individual and unique cultures. That will be a continuing challenge during the next twenty-five years and beyond.

EDUCATION

Education will be for all, and third-level education will be for all who require it. Developments since the 1990s will ensure that education will be for living as well as for work. The thirst for education will be greater than at any time in history and continuing education or lifelong learning, whether necessitated by employment or as an added quality to life, will be very much the norm.

Engineering and science will have a prominent place, but engineering and science will be taught within a spectrum which embraces much more of the humanities and social sciences as people continue to recognise that technology must be balanced by other viewpoints and that the continuous impact of imported information must also be countered by an ability for individuals and national populations to think for themselves. The philosophy of education in the year 2020 will be different from the philosophy of the 1990s, with initial education forming 'the first module' for lifelong learning.

Radical changes will have occurred in curricula of courses at second- and third-level. In third-level, in particular, all courses will take account of the new information and technological age, and humanities will be leavened by the sciences and the sciences will be leavened by the humanities, as education becomes more integrated to better serve the needs of society. In engineering education, the idea of a 'fixed set of facts to be learned, tested and rewarded' will certainly no longer be the case. An expanded engineering education will ensure that engineers will be enabled to provide a comprehensive service which an increasingly technological society and a questioning and demanding public will continue to seek. Engineering courses will become broader, and complementary studies in management, finance, economics, social awareness, environmental and business ethics will be very much a part of an expanded curriculum.

Education technology will remove much of the drudgery of teaching and learning and the Internet and the capacity of computer systems to give access to and store data will give students and teachers an almost unlimited resource of valuable information.

An important aspect of education for students at first- second- and third-level will be the rational teaching of universal history. A world which since World War II has seen innumerable wars, which were based on greed, corruption, arrogant nationalism and the accumulated hates of long-gone generations will have realised that national history aligned to the universal history of the peoples of the world will contribute in no small way towards greater and more rational understanding among peoples worldwide. This will be of significant importance to a forward-looking Ireland.

QUALITY INDUSTRY

Irish industry will be as much a part of the information age as any other country. Ireland has always kept pace with the best in this regard and the development of new technologies will not leave Ireland behind. Government efforts towards increasing industrialisation will still bear fruit and an increasingly highly educated technological workforce will more than treble during the next twenty-five years. This will ensure that Ireland will be as well placed to serve national and multinational business as any other country in the world.

Ireland's marketing abroad will also be stepped up to the extent that the Irish sales forces overseas will have a well-deserved reputation for competence and a reputation second to none for being able to deliver. This will be a major objective for all governments to achieve in the intervening years.

In every aspect of Irish business the concentration in the coming decades will be to emphasise quality to the stage that Irish quality will be synonymous with what we have come to regard as Swiss or German quality. It will be a major selling point and in situations where cheaper labour forces may produce cheaper goods Irish competitiveness will depend, to a large extent, on the quality product. The slogan for 2020 could well be: 'Think Quality – Teach Quality – Produce Quality – Sell Quality Irish.'

Programmes of government will ensure that continuing emphasis will be placed on Irish design, Irish production methods, Irish quality control and Irish marketing, whatever the product. Ireland will be competing aggressively in software production, the export of services, communications technology and in mechanical engineering where very high quality precision engineering, for instance, will be in increasing demand and very appropriate for high-tech Irish manufacture.

The management of business, such as has made other countries pre-eminent in the latter end of the twentieth century, will be brought far more to the fore in the Ireland of the twenty-first century, as professionalism and qualifications for management are better recognised. By the year 2020 a cadre of first-class managers will underpin the success of Irish business.

A greatly increased technological labour force will mean that Ireland will have a technology bias which will continue to increase. A small home market will mean an ever-increasing demand for an export market and Irish engineers, scientists, manufacturers and exporters will all speak the languages of the global market on the basis that if you can't speak to them you can't sell to them.

Additionally, the policies of government will be far more technologically driven than they were in the previous century.

The lessons will have been learned from the case of Singapore and other countries which developed rapidly in the latter end of the twentieth century. At that time in Singapore, for instance, some 50% of the cabinet were engineers and 75% of senior civil servants were also engineers. That arose from a defined policy of government to establish Singapore as a small country with a pre-eminent position in business and manufacturing, and it succeeded. Ireland will have used that and other examples to great effect.

DEVELOPMENT AND CONSTRUCTION

The major developments in Ireland, particularly during the decade of the 1990s, brought the infrastructure of the country into the twenty-first century and in the first decade of the new century this process of new construction and development will continue. However, in the second and third decade of the new century, the problem for Ireland will be the maintenance of the infrastructure that was put in place over the previous thirty to fifty years. Major investment in development took little account of the investments necessary to maintain an expanded infrastructure. That will be a major drain on national finances in 2020 and is something which will add considerably to the burden of taxation by that year.

A national road infrastructure, which in the 1990s had twice as much surfaced road per head of the population as many other developed countries, will continue to be a significant part of national infrastructural costs. Even with a gradual process of abandonment of less-used roads, maintenance of motorways, and regional and county roads will become a major problem for government by the year 2020.

In like manner, the deterioration of many of the structures built in the 1950s, 1960s and 1970s will be a constant source of cost in the new century and will be a spur towards ongoing research into new materials, better design and better construction for better maintenance for the future.

Development of the infrastructure will not stop in 2020. It will continue, and communication and power facilities, roads, harbours, airports will continue to be constructed or upgraded in line with the demands of an expanding economy.

Sanitary services will continue to improve and upgrading of water supplies, including the rehabilitation of the older water distribution systems, will have been completed to the extent that even with increased demand and irrespective of climatic conditions, water supply in Ireland will be adequate and to the highest quality.

The development of regional airports as private or public enterprises will continue as a vital adjunct to export business and as an important service to a mobile Irish international workforce which will continue to have their homes in Ireland.

RESEARCH AND DEVELOPMENT

Ireland's low investment in research and development in the latter part of the twentieth century will be perceived to have been a serious mistake and not in tune with government policy to expand Irish technology. The early years of the twenty-first century will see a significant increase in research and development in Ireland as the objective of producing quality Irish and innovative Irish goods is pursued. The philosophy of depending on the ingenuity of others to produce what we need for indigenous industry will gradually take second place to a philosophy of Irish research for Irish development for Irish industry. The increasing resource of engineering and scientific manpower will be enabled to avail of, and contribute significantly to, such research, which will naturally have substantial international links.

TOURISM AND ENVIRONMENT

Tourism will be one of the most significant national revenue earners and an even more significant employer. Ireland's advantages for quality and cultural tourism will be realised to a greater extent than ever before. Significant investment will be made in the early years of the new century to enhance everything which contributes to Ireland's uniqueness for tourism. Recognising the extraordinary competition which other developed countries pose to each other in attracting tourism, Ireland will have developed what it can do best. In this regard, the Irish environment, including the cleanliness of our seas and estuaries, the preservation and enhancement of our landscape, the provision of first-class accommodation, the highest standards of cleanliness and order throughout our towns, villages, countryside and coastal regions, the ease of access and the availability of information on our cultural sites and the development of our education and music will all be supported to an extent hardly conceived of at the end of the twentieth century. This will be a major national drive and the education of our people at all levels on the environment and in environmental concern will be a continuing process, which will be yielding significant fruit in the year 2020.

Ireland will be another Switzerland. The Swiss have been using this approach for a long time and in the years leading up to 2020 a similarly professional approach here will ensure the future of tourism as a major business and the preservation of our environment as one of our most precious and significant selling points.

Special emphasis will be placed on our relatively unspoilt coastal regions where continuous erosion control, the protection of sand dunes and the most rigorous development controls will give Ireland a unique resource in 2020 and beyond.

AGRICULTURE AND FOOD

Irish agribusiness, which has shown that it can compete with the best, will still be our major industry in the year 2020. Ireland's food industry, because of its quality standards and the environment from which it is produced, will, with proper professional marketing, have as large a place in world markets as Denmark or New Zealand. The emphasis at all times will be on quality and purity. Processing in Ireland will have been the goal of government in the decades leading up to 2020 and our ability to supply markets overseas will be matched by an ability to feed ourselves. This will be a major input to national finances and a very definite move away from the import of produce which could as well be produced at home given the right conditions, proper husbandry and adequate support.

The production of organic foods will be an important aspect of Irish agriculture. Production and export will benefit greatly from increasing world appreciation of organically produced products.

Agricultural and food engineering will play a major role in conjunction with the food science in the development of Ireland's food industry into the next century and the impact of high-tech instrumentation and better communication systems which will be introduced into Irish agriculture and food during the early decades of the twenty-first century, will make Ireland's agriculture and food industry pre-eminent in the world.

High-tech application of fertilisers and pesticides will reduce the deleterious effects of such additives as well as increasing the efficiency of use. This will have a remarkable spin-off with regard to limitation of discharge of nutrients and pesticides to rivers, lakes and estuaries from agriculture.

The development of systems of slurry disposal and new systems of animal husbandry will, by the year 2020, have eliminated much potential damage which mishandled or misapplied slurry could cause to the environment. The marketability of the by-products from such disposal systems will have long been realised and a substantial business will have been built up in the production of stable, uniform and odour-free organic fertiliser.

TRANSPORT

In the year 2020 road transport will still be the major mode of transportation, although rail transport will expand as new and cheaper systems of electric light rail will be developed with the possibility of the re-opening of many of the old railway rights of way, which will have been preserved by government on the basis that they could be used by future transport modes not yet developed.

In 2020 policies of limitation on the growth of cities and the increasingly popular movement of populations to smaller urban and rural locations will alter attitudes to transport. The superhighway will encourage such relocation and working from home will be very much the norm for many who will prefer to live and work away from 'the madding crowd's ignoble strife'.

Transportation in the cities will be greatly changed, with severely restricted movement of private cars throughout the centre of cities and sophisticated systems of public transport, either light rail, guided bus or other modes of transport not yet developed, very much the vogue.

The private car user will accept as a fact of life, that unlimited access to the private car will not be available and that first-class public transport in cities and towns will be widespread, available, acceptable and cheap.

National and international pressure on car manufacturers, and increasing use of on-board computers will lead to the development of 'intelligent' cars, which apart from aiding the driver, will also make a large contribution to reducing the slaughter on the roads.

Air and sea transport will continue to grow. There will not be a land link between Northern Ireland and Scotland but high-speed ferries and cheap, efficient and frequent air shuttles between Britain and Ireland and between the Continent and Ireland will establish those links which are so necessary to an exporting economy. The ability of the travelling Irish to return home frequently will be a feature of the 2020s and will help reverse the trend of depopulation in our countryside which was a feature up to the end of 1990s.

ENERGY – THE LIFE SUPPORT OF MODERN SOCIETY

The likelihood is that by the year 2020 one or two serious energy crises will have occurred as instability in the Middle East and the drying-up of oil reserves put increasing pressure on the development of alternatives and on energy prices. It is probable that by then, with the costs of energy increasing, Ireland will be enabled to exploit the modest reserves off our shores and, by the year 2020, Ireland may be self-sufficient in very expensive oil. However, all pressures nationally and internationally will be to combat the greenhouse effect and the diminution of the ozone layer. Strict national and international controls will have been imposed on all emissions and particularly those from fossil fuels, whether from cars, power stations or domestic systems. Considerable investment will be necessary to reduce such emissions, which will add significantly to the costs to business and individual customers. Natural gas, which will continue to be available either from national or international sources, will be a major power source, and will be Ireland's principal approach to clean energy. Otherwise in the burning of fossil fuels, Ireland and other countries around the world will be bound by the various protocols to reduce CO_2 and SO_2 emissions progressively.

Conservation will also be the policy of all into the next century as the world faces continuing depletion of fossil fuel resources prior to the onset of other systems, whether fusion, fission, or other alternatives.

The impact of alternative energy sources – wind and wave power and bio-fuels in particular – will be very much on the national energy agenda but it is unlikely that such alternative sources will account for more than 10% of our total energy demand in 2020. Subsequently, however, there will be an accelerated development as technology improves particularly in generation from wave and wind.

GOVERNMENT

A number of aspects of the year 2020 have been highlighted. All have been highlighted with the idea that certain parameters will be achieved. Those parameters include a strengthening world order, relative peace throughout the world, an expanded and generally united European Union and sensible trading arrangements between the great world trading blocs.

This forecast also pre-supposes strong governments in Ireland dedicated to leadership and development, with the country coming before party. This may be a pipe dream, but the increasing sophistication and intolerance of an educated population will, by the early decades of the next century, ensure that governments are elected with genuine vision and a sense of patriotism towards the development of their own country, within the wider international family and with the strength to achieve results.

Such governments will lead and not be lobby led. Such governments will have the support of the people to make decisions and not be afraid to make unpopular decisions. The management of national finances will be subject to the closest scrutiny and will not allow for over-spend. It is also likely that new technology will give the people the ability to agree or not to agree important issues by frequent referenda, which will be part of a sophisticated system of government giving everyone a genuine say in national decision-making.

The Oireachtas will be smaller, more efficient and more accountable and radical reforms in government and local administration will ensure that the management of the affairs of the country is efficiently carried out and that waste of effort and money will not be the norm twenty-five years from now.

THE NORTH

By the year 2020, a new generation, more pragmatic, better educated and more conscious of their role in a country which has citizenship of a wider community will have all but abandoned the shibboleths of the past in Northern Ireland. The late 1990s and the early decade of the new millennium will not see a diminution of divisions, but diminish they will as other times and other people move into the decision-making process. The government of Ireland in 2020 could be in the form of regionalised assemblies contributing to a new 'slimline' Oireachtas with well-defined powers, nationally and internationally.

The hope expressed by Tom Kettle, the Irish soldier poet, for the North in the early part of the twentieth century, may well come true twenty years into the new millennium:

> No rudest man who died
>
> To tear your flag down in the bitter years
>
> But shall have praise, and three times thrice again
>
> When at the table men shall drink with men

CULTURE

Ireland is different and will remain so. The communication revolution will affect us and may tend to swamp us. However, there is an individuality in the Irish character which, in spite of all, has survived. The reaction of the Irish people to the import of foreign culture, whether by Internet or otherwise, will be great and by the year 2020 Ireland will be more Irish, more national, more culturally aware of its heritage, language, literature and music than at any time in the previous century. It will not reject the new era of communication but will develop and protect its own culture and identity and be conscious that an ethnic difference adds colour to our character and makes us unique in what we are.

Part of that culture will be the traditional adherence of Irish people to their religious faith. That inherent sense of spirituality, which is as much a part of our ethnic identity as any other, will grow and strengthen throughout the succeeding years of the new millennium. People in 2020 will recognise that strong churches with an unequivocal voice for morality and leading by example will be pillars of the society that will exist twenty-five years from now.

Having written the above, I am reminded of De Valera's much misquoted and often unjustly maligned vision of Ireland, given in a radio broadcast in 1943:

> A land whose countryside would be bright with cosy homesteads, whose fields and villages would be joyous with the sound of industry, with the romping of sturdy children, the contests of athletic youths, the laughter of comely maidens, whose firesides would be forums for serene old age.

Not a bad vision when all is said and done. If we can achieve it by 2020, we won't be doing badly!

Eileen O'Mara

Planning for a World of Change

Eileen O'Mara Walsh is chairwoman of Forbairt, managing director of O'Mara Travel Ltd and Heritage Island Ltd, and director of Great Southern Hotels.

Most forecasting, even if you are a budding HG Wells, is in practice little more than an extrapolation of existing trends. We extend the technological and consumer trends that we already recognise as dynamic, throw in a few variables like demographic factors and likely competitive behaviour, do some number-crunching and then dilute the results if the gap between the present and the forecast future seems too difficult to come to terms with!

On a five-year or a ten-year time-scale, such an approach can often be adequate. The challenge of the present exercise is to take a twenty-five year view, a time-scale of a totally different order. A period of twenty-five years is more than enough for whole industrial sectors to die and be forgotten, more than enough for entirely new, at present unthought-of, sectors to be born, to establish themselves, and indeed to become dominant.

The 'dinosaur risk' is of finding yourself locked in a doomed battle against inexorable forces. This can be because a product or service is simply not needed any more – because, for instance, technology has made it obsolete. Or it can be because the product or service can be produced on a cost basis with which you can no longer hope to compete.

Sometimes, of course, even these situations can provide opportunities. An obsolete product or service can have a future if it tailors itself to a different set of needs; we don't use horses and carriages as a means of transport today but the spruced up barouches, hansom cabs and sidecars spanking along St Stephen's Green are testimony to our ability to successfully target a niche market and – incidentally – another aspect of creativity in Irish tourism.

Equally, businesses whose original custom is threatened or has been wiped out by low-cost competitors can sometimes create a new place for themselves by concentrating on quality and high added value. For instance, yesterday's mass textile business may transform itself into tomorrow's high-fashion businesses, where the will and the capability to adapt exists together with the determination to take on the challenge of sourcing out new markets.

Interestingly enough, the qualities needed to find opportunities within the dinosaur scenario are much the same as those needed to exploit the opportunities that arise from completely new directions. Among these qualities are openness to the possibility of change, and flexibility in responding to the needs of change.

Openness to change is a prerequisite because we, as human beings, crave stability and continuity. We have an inbuilt tendency to deny the reality of change, even when by objective standards it is staring us in the face. We want to believe the future is going to be like the past, with no more than a few cosmetic trimmings. Our instinct is to be closed to change.

My vision for 2020, and my hope, is that we in Ireland can surmount these instincts, which are reinforced in our case by some of our traditions and much of our history.

We need, as a small country that will always have to fight for its place in the economic world, to be enthusiastic embracers of change – not people who are dragged along, tardily and reluctantly, in the wake of others.

We may not, of course, have the clout to initiate major technological change ourselves – but that is not the point. The point is that we have to be abreast of change, whenever it is initiated. We have to be capable of recognising the forces of change, and we have to become faster and more skilled at recognising the implications for Ireland (good and bad) of new developments as soon as they arise.

We need to develop this openness to change at all levels.

- individual companies need it, and perhaps need to be encouraged and helped towards it;
- development agencies such as Forbairt must be driven by it, because if we are not the catalysts of change we become part of the problem rather than part of the solution;
- at the highest national level, the level of government and administration, it is vital that our planning is approached on the assumption that change is the norm, not the exception;
- equally, this embracing of change must extend also to the general public, it needs to become a part of our national psyche.

However, it is only one part of the story.

Flexibility in the face of change is just as important. It is not enough to recognise change, not enough to recognise its implications. We have also to act. To benefit from the opportunities of change, we have also to change ourselves. To change what we offer the market-place in response to changing needs and changing competitive pressures; to change the technology we use to produce and deliver our products and services; to change, too, the way we work and organise ourselves.

From the perspective of 2020, it is important for us to realise now that many of our institutions are based not on an assumption of change but of stability.

Education, for instance, still suffers from the hangover of a view that saw the early part of a person's life being spent in acquiring knowledge, knowledge which was then applied during the remainder of the person's lifetime.

The emphasis was on transferring knowledge in the form of facts, or on transferring highly-specific skills that were tailored to discrete activities that were not expected to change very much over an individual's career.

To educate like this for the world of 2020 would be like training dinosaurs for extinction. The facts of today will be out-of-date tomorrow. The specific skills of today will be obsolete tomorrow. Education for 2020 needs to take a world of constant change as a given. It needs to focus on developing skills that will equip people to adapt continuously to the changes they will face again and again throughout their lives.

Management, too, has traditionally been based on continuity rather than change.

Most managers have seen their central task as being to manage what is there, what exists now. In the future that will largely be a technological function.

But the future role of management, and indeed of people generally in business activity, will be to initiate and carry through the constant changes that will be necessary to keep a company successful in an environment that is in a state of continuous flux.

Change will not be just an occasional challenge that companies have to face from time to time, but the central challenge that a company and its people face on a daily basis.

It will be clear from what has gone before that my focus in looking forward to the year 2020 is more on how I hope we will behave than on the actual nature of the world we will then face. There is a vast agenda for us in becoming open to change, and in becoming sufficiently flexible to cope with it. These are the overriding tasks that should shape our approach to the very long term.

At the same time, however, it can be useful to do some old-fashioned crystal-ball gazing, because it can give us some kind of early warning of at least some of the opportunities and threats. I propose here to touch on just two of the opportunities.

Emerging changes in the way people and companies work open tremendous opportunities for Ireland.

A number of trends, some of which are interconnected, are potentially a means of adding to our strengths and of over-coming traditional weaknesses.

One obvious one is the increasing dominance of telecommunications as the medium of communication. This favours Ireland because it reduces the negative factor that our relatively remote location has always been. In a telematic age, location is already almost irrelevant; by 2020, location will be *completely* irrelevant. Instead of people moving to find work, work can come to them along fibre-optic cables.

On the international scene, this allows us to perform services for people outside our borders. We are already seeing the possibilities for Ireland in this, in high value-added areas such as financial services and telemarketing. However, as the costs of telecoms fall and the quality and range of telematic possibilities extends, the scope of the opportunities in internationally traded services is likely to develop exponentially.

Up to now, the benefits to Ireland have come from attracting international companies to operate international service activities from a location in this country. By the year 2020, I hope we will have a thriving sector made up mainly of Irish companies who have identified and developed opportunities in this area – and who will provide a substantial proportion of the country's jobs. It is highly likely that most of the Irish multinationals of the future will operate in the world of services rather than in manufacturing.

But, of course, the impact of the telematics age is not only on our trading relationship with the outside world, vitally important though that is. It also has the potential to make changes within Ireland which are highly desirable.

It was, after all, the industrial revolution that created modern cities as we know them. Today's cities grew up because of the nature of the work that the industrial era demanded. It is not too fanciful to speculate that the telematics revolution could eventually provoke an equally radical shift – but in exactly the opposite direction.

If it does not matter where in the world you work, by extension it does not matter where in Ireland you work. If it is as practical to produce a product or a service in a remote rural area as it is in an urban or a city environment, some of the imbalance between town and country will be removed. Similarly, if education, medical and entertainment services can be delivered at equal cost and quality anywhere in the country, the balance of the quality of life will also tend to shift.

This may seem to paint an unduly rosy picture of the prospects for regional development, particularly in the light of the trends of past decades, but there are other developments apart from telematics that would tend to support it.

We are already seeing in industrial organisations a marked trend towards interdependence between business units, rather than the almost total dependence on the centre that characterised the past. The growth of out-sourcing is creating opportunities for smaller companies, both in manufacturing and in services. Technology has made it possible for very small groups of people to deliver what would once have demanded a much larger organisation.

So, running in parallel with the evident need for great scale in some industrial activities is the growing potential for smaller companies – companies which can deliver a high quality product or service to bigger companies which are concentrating their energies on activities that are core to them.

In 2020 there will, I believe, be a very important role for smaller

Irish companies. But these will be companies delivering a standard of quality and professionalism and of strategic vision that is at least on a par with the largest organisations now. The demands on small companies will grow in step with the opportunities that open up for them.

The second area of opportunity that I want to touch on has to do with the area of activity in which I have personally spent most of my working life – tourism. Ireland has the opportunity to cash in hugely from the emerging world trends in leisure and tourism.

For starters let me look back at the travel scene in the Ireland of twenty-five years ago before setting my telescopic sights at the year 2020.

In 1970 I was a youthful enthusiast in the business of travel and tourism for the under-thirties, myself a product of the sixties generation, full of impatience and certainty for the start of a new golden age. That was before the oil crisis, inflation and the *real politik* of 'greed is good' brought in 'yuppiedom' to replace our wide-eyed hunger for revolution.

Back then the innovative package deal of J1 work visas plus cheap transatlantic charters brought about a mass exodus of a generation of students, swopping the canning factories of the North of England for the fast and furious buck of the New York construction and bar trade. In the opposite direction came the long-haired, long-limbed students of UCLA, Yale and some not so Ivy League establishments, to demand more of Irish tourism than kissing the Blarney Stone – to seek out Yeats and Joyce and, along with their European counterparts, to force feed the invention of budget accommodation.

Around the same time the first wave of Irish holiday-makers had hit the beaches of the Costa del Sol and the sophisticated were tasting the more hedonistic delights of Club Med in Greece.

Electric typewriters and instant communication by telex led to my own technological baptism of fire when it took four strong men to carry our first main-frame computer up two flights of stairs to our office.

Twenty-five years on, what's new? Club Med has come to Co. Kerry, the telex has been banished to the basement, fax, modems, compuserve, Internet and mobile phones dominate our lives but the prophesies of doom that the microchip would replace people have been proved wrong. Travel and tourism now employ more than 100,000 people in Ireland, account for 6% of GNP and are predicted to be the world's greatest industry long before the year 2020. But it will not be the tourism of the past.

Neither does it mean, however, that Ireland has to become a mass tourism destination. To do so would be to kill off the very product that is our central attraction – a high quality, protected environment, providing a peaceful destination with an unhurried pace of life that encourages relaxation and reflection and a wealth of very pleasant activities.

For one thing, different work patterns mean that more people will take several breaks – perhaps shorter ones – throughout the year, rather than the traditional two weeks in the summer.

For another, an increasing amount of the wealth generated by tourism and trade will be goal directed. People will use their breaks to do things, discover things, to explore things. The idea of a holiday whose purpose was solely to relax, with perhaps a genuflection towards sightseeing, is well on the way to extinction.

Ireland is, potentially, superbly placed to take advantage of these trends. But as in all forms of business activity in the next century, realising the potential will demand very radical change.

For instance:

- it may well be that the traditional concept of the package tour is not geared to the opportunities of the future. We need to make sure we are not designing accommodation and products for an age that has past;
- cultural tourism, perhaps the fastest emerging hot trend,

is a long, long way from the superficiality of traditional sight-seeing. We need to make sure that we are alive to the difference, and begin to adjust what we offer to the new needs.

But above all, we need as a nation to adjust to the implications of an economy where tourism and leisure account for perhaps three times as much of our GNP as they do now. The history of our approach to business over the past fifty years has been to play up the importance of manufacturing and play down the importance of services including tourism.

In 2020, services of all kinds will provide the overwhelming majority of jobs. Manufacturing will continue to be critically important to us, but its role may well have developed into one where it will create wealth for the economy but relatively few jobs.

Our national aims in regard to providing jobs for our people, here in the country of their birth, will increasingly be realised by the services sector. To thrive in the environment of the future, we will have to see ourselves principally as the providers of high quality services – to each other, and to the world.

From my vantage point midway between 1970 and 2020 I position myself as a mix of old fogey and visionary – I believe if we can harness technology and retain personal service we can make tangible that most intangible of products 'the dream holiday'. Whether it is watching the sun set over a Connemara bog or the sun rise over the Nile, I can't and won't accept that Virtual Reality will replace personal experience be it in the year 2010 or 2020 – except perhaps for those who prefer Sun City to the real Africa. I also predict that in 2020 my son's grandchildren will read the printed page as well as, or maybe even in preference to, the computer screen. They will laugh out loud at *Winnie the Pooh* and cry at Jane Eyre's treatment at the hands of the awful Brocklehurst, and that *Casablanca* will still be the favourite film of all time!

Padraic A White

Post-Colonial Ireland Comes of Age

Padraic A White was managing director of the Irish Development Authority (IDA Ireland) from 1981 to 1990, and is now chairman of BRW Insurance and Financial Services group.

In the year 2020, some twenty-five years away, the greater number of the people of Ireland will be planning commemorations, and in many cases celebrations, to mark the following year's centenary of the founding of the Irish Free State in 1921, signifying the end of long centuries of colonial rule over the island of Ireland.

It also took twenty-five years from the outbreak in 1969 of political violence on the island to the declaration of a ceasefire in autumn 1994 and a commitment to a peace process which the majority of people want desperately to succeed. In those twenty-five years, there were over 3,000 related deaths, many more maimed for life, there was fear and insecurity and immense destruction of property.

Over a year later, the peace process and ceasefire are still in place, despite many testing and anxious times in the first year.

We speak nowadays of the need to accord 'parity of esteem' to both traditions in Ireland, of respect for the nationalist and unionist traditions and of finding a historically new way for the divided peoples of Ireland to live in harmony with each other.

There is a better than even chance that when the year 2020

dawns, the people of Northern Ireland will have the experience of political harmony and will have devised innovative political structures to sustain it. One generation in Northern Ireland missed out on peace and having tasted the joy, relief and the lack of personal fear of the first year of the ceasefire, it is hard to imagine that parents will allow the next generation to suffer the same fate.

I have opened this essay with the prospects for peace in Northern Ireland because peace on the island, or lack of it, or renewed strife will have a pervasive influence on all aspects of life, including the business sector, and on the quality and texture of our personal lives.

In the days of the Empire, it was said that 'trade follows the flag'. Equally in modern Ireland, business prospects will be heavily influenced by the political evolution of the island and between the island and the European Union.

There is a second reason for dwelling on the politics and history of Ireland. During a career devoted to promoting Irish enterprise, I have been profoundly impressed by the persistence of traits, characteristics and attitudes into contemporary business life that come from the experience of being a colonised people. In the new Irish state post-1921, the public sector was seen by the Catholic population as the one with prestige, status and security. The limited private sector was largely in the hands of the Protestant and Anglo-Irish families: the brewing and distilling companies, the big stores, the stockbrokers, the rural provender mills.

The main centre of international class industry – shipbuilding, engineering and textiles – was cut off from the new state by partition of the island.

The Act of Union of 1800 which forced a small nascent economy into a common market with the powerful pioneer of the Industrial Revolution destroyed many young industries such as glass crystal and silverware.

The policy of protection and encouragement of native industries by high tariffs and import restrictions during the forty years preceding entry to the European Union in 1973 bred a limited native industrial tradition where customer choice and care, and product or service quality, received little attention.

We are only now beginning to perceive the emergence of a distinctive and creative business culture in the Republic of Ireland. It is being powered by a young generation who are more educated and more international in experience; by a determined and creative small business sector committed to quality; and by a small number of pioneering native international companies combined with a much greater number of foreign companies serving Europe from Ireland.

The shift is now underway from a culture dominated by the state and its bureaucracy towards a more entrepreneurial society. This shift is well symbolised by the political consensus that personal taxes cannot be increased. The citizenry consider they are entitled to keep the majority of their personal earnings rather than have them docked at source by the state under PAYE.

The Republic is in an historic transition from a rigid centralised hierarchical society to one whose shape and texture is hard to divine. There is a sense that the old order is collapsing: the historically high fertility rate has halved in the past thirty years (from 4 per 1,000 in 1965 to 1.93 in 1993) the national media report that 'poll finds Irish losing faith faster than rest of EU states' (*Irish Times*, 28 July 1995); two referenda in a decade – 1986 and 1995 – focus on the removal of the constitutional ban on divorce and re-marriage.

It is reasonable to predict that the new order will be more entrepreneurial, more diverse, more individualistic and more international in orientation. There will be a distinctively Irish blend to the new order, influenced strongly by the extent of interaction with Northern Ireland, which will distinguish it from other European countries.

If there is a dark side, it could come from the communal impact of extensive substance abuse – drugs and alcohol – and their adverse effects on personal life, business careers and crime and violence in the society.

These changes will shape the leaders and the environment for business in Ireland and will now be considered more closely.

THE NEW GENERATION IS HERE

The new generation which will shape most of the next twenty-five years is already born and we can discern fairly clearly the demographic shifts in this period.

The impact of young people in the twenties age group, (that is ages twenty to twenty-nine inclusive) will be the most striking feature.

Ireland will be coming to terms with a shrinking child and teenage population and this in itself will change the social landscape from the familiar one of play spaces and footpaths bustling with children. By the year 2020, there are likely to be between 250,000 and 400,000 less children and teenagers than in 1991, depending primarily on whether relatively high fertility rates or a continuation of present declining trends are assumed.[1]

The twenties age group has been growing rapidly, reflecting the high fertility rates of the decade 1970-80, and the number in that age group increased by some 60,000 in the past five years to an estimated present level of 570,000. They will be a highly influential segment of the population, of the order of 500,000, in the year 2020.[2]

They are, in the main, starting their careers at this age and for the first time earning their own spending money.

With the resumption of fast economic growth in the Republic in 1994 (7.4% GNP), and an historically high expansion of employment, their influence on business and social life in Ireland is more and more evident.

For example, the companies licensed for the International Financial Services Centre in Dublin employ some two thousand in highly specialised services who are part of a genuinely global financial market. They are well paid. A significant number have returned from the financial centres of London and New York to be part of this emerging Ireland.

This youth generation is also strongly represented among the 'hidden Ireland' of the ninety thousand people who are at the heart of the one thousand foreign manufacturing and international service companies based in Ireland and serving European or world markets. They are part of the most advanced management and technological companies in the world, yet their companies are only now being publicly accepted as a permanent and enduring feature of Ireland's business landscape. These Young Irelanders are, for example, engaged in making the most sophisticated microprocessors in the world at Intel's fabrication plant in Leixlip, Co. Kildare.

It is this new generation which is also now beginning to shape social life in Ireland: in café society, in the media and the arts.

And they are not simply young – they are in the main exceptionally well educated and this is going to be an even more influential factor in the next twenty years.

In the 1980s, the Industrial Development Authority (IDA Ireland), of which I was managing director, adopted the promotional theme of 'Ireland – Home of the Young Europeans' as the most powerful differentiating attraction of Ireland for international investors.

It was chosen after extensive research and reflection which concluded that, compared with other European locations, the preponderance in Ireland of young people who were well educated was likely to be the country's most powerful attraction for the international companies in the knowledge- and technology-based industries.

It proved to be a highly effective promotion since business leaders themselves came more and more to focus on the 'quality of our people' as the key to business success.

The trends in higher education are truly remarkable. In the past three decades, the numbers in higher education expanded almost five-fold from nineteen thousand in 1965 to eighty-eight thousand in 1993 and there were still some ten thousand qualified applicants who failed annually to get a place in recent years. The escalating demand reflects the traditionally high esteem accorded to education in Ireland and the recognition by a rising young population and their parents that higher educational qualifications increase the prospects of well-paid employment. The demand for, and supply of, higher education places is likely to increase substantially in future years. The Higher Education Authority has recommended that planning for the higher education sector should proceed on the basis of 118,000 students in the year 2015, that is, almost one-third up on the 1993 level.[3] The participation rate of young people in higher education would by then have risen from 40% to 54% in 2015.

Furthermore, the increasingly educated young population are far more mobile internationally than any previous generation. They avail of low-cost airfares and ease of travel to move abroad for new experiences or jobs and back to Ireland, without the heartbreak and sense of finality of previous generations. New data casts fresh light on these movements. Thus, in the four years 1991-94, when net emigration did not exceed 10,000 in any year, there was very heavy in-migration to Ireland in the range of 30,000 to 40,000 each year.

The Central Statistics Office (CSO) report confirms that: 'A significant proportion of the inward flows is accounted for by Irish persons returning after a period of living abroad.'[4]

The indications are that this generation can exploit the global village but that the call of their native land brings them back, increasingly so, as their peers are forming a critical and influential mass in Irish society and business and as the Republic's economy is sustaining average growth of 4%-5% per annum.

FUTURE SHOCK
THE IMPACT OF WOMEN IN BUSINESS AND POLITICS

Within the overall social change, the growing power of women stands out as likely to carry the greatest impact on the way business and politics is conducted in Ireland. The manifestations of this future shock are abundant and visible. Women's participation in the labour force has increased in recent years and is expected to grow at more than twice the corresponding rate for men over the next ten years: 2% per annum in the period 1994-2006 compared with 0.8% for men.[5]

Participation by married women will show the greatest gain, at 3.2% per annum in the period, adding further to the rate of social change.

Detailed occupational employment studies and forecasts give us insights into the drama which is now taking place in the workplace and likely to continue.[6] The FÁS/ESRI study comments that 'the five areas in which the female share of total employment is expected to increase fastest in the medium term are in what are considered typically male occupations.'

These five areas are of the predicted share of women in each category in 1998: business, finance and legal professionals (37%); higher managers (24%); brokers and agents (26%); foremen and supervisors (18%); labourers (4%).

The dramatic change underway is shown, for example, by the fact that only twenty years ago, women represented less than 5% of higher managers, but by 1998, that proportion will have increased five-fold to some 24%.

Reinforcing the perception of a substantially enhanced role for women in the workplace will be rapid declines in occupations traditionally associated with women, namely, packing and bottling, clothing and textiles.

Underpinning these changes is the revolution in women's participation in education.

In the past thirty years, women's participation in higher education has moved from 31% to 49% or virtual equality today.[7] Analysis of Leaving Certificate results shows that girls out-perform boys in the main subjects. Thus, in 1994 girls did better in nine out of the ten most popular higher level papers in the Leaving Certificate – only in accounting did boys fare slightly better.[8]

The greater flexibility of work patterns – part-time, sub-contracting, self-employment – compared with the traditional monolithic model of the whole-time job, has also enabled women to maintain their links to the workplace after marriage. The incidence of part-time employment is still low (7.5% in 1992) but will move rapidly to the EU average of 13%, with the great majority of the part-time jobs being taken by women.

These changes, though quite revolutionary in extent, have not had a significant impact yet on the way business is conducted in Ireland. In most boardrooms and at most business meetings, women are scarcely, if at all, represented. The dominant business mores are still the traditional male ones. The reason I regard women's enhanced participation in business as a crucial future issue is that I believe it will lead to profound changes in the way business is conducted and in the actual ethos and operation of companies. The crucial turning point will come when women reach a critical mass at the higher levels of organisations, probably around 30% of the staff.

The male-dominated business world is not prepared for the changes in store: hence the likelihood of future shock.

Similar considerations apply to women in parliament, and

hence with access to political power. Women account for a modest 13% of elected Dáil members in Ireland, over 20% in Germany and Austria and over 30% in the Scandinavian countries.[9] In view of the speed of social change in Ireland, and the predicted enhancement of women's participation and influence, an Irish figure in the range of 25% to 30% by the year 2020 is judged to be eminently feasible.

THE PEACE DIVIDEND

The political divisions between Northern Ireland and the Republic and the lack of normal cooperation between the two parts of the island has resulted in two neighbouring economies with an unnaturally low level of linkage between them. The Northern economy remained overwhelmingly oriented to the UK, and sourcing of goods and supplies by firms from across the political border remained exceptionally low.

In recent years, there has been an increase in cross-border business acquisitions, particularly by southern companies in sectors such as drug distribution and retailing.

Business-to-business contacts have been increasing for some years and the ceasefire has given a new impetus to these contacts.

The business traditions and strengths in Northern Ireland are very different to those in the Republic. There is undoubtedly a considerable economic dynamic to be released by greater real business links and synergy between the business sectors on the island, given peace and stability in political relations.

The main initial beneficiaries of the peace are likely to be tourism and related investment, and inward investment.

There is already evidence since the autumn 1994 ceasefire of significant joint business involvement in the tourism/hotel sector (eg, Merrion Hotel, Dublin).

There is international goodwill towards Ireland from an international business community impressed by the achievement of peace after a twenty-five year bitter struggle.

Both North and South have highly professional investment promotion agencies (IDB, Northern Ireland; IDA Ireland) and there is the potential for greater investment benefits to both from combining together to promote the island of Ireland.

The comparative advantage in both parts of Ireland will be based on promoting knowledge-intensive industries based on an educated and committed workforce, first-class supporting services, such as telecoms, and supportive government and public attitudes. As political cooperation evolves, so will the logic and mutual benefits from more concerted international investment promotion manifest themselves.

As mutual trust develops on the island, there will emerge many projects which carry clear additional mutual benefits if undertaken jointly or in a concerted manner. The re-opening of the Erne-Shannon waterway is one example already completed. The proposal for an Economic Corridor on the Belfast-Dublin route is another such project.

CONCLUSION

This paper has touched on strategic changes over the next twenty-five years which are judged to have a profound impact on life and on business on the island of Ireland. Two questions on which a good outcome rests must remain on the table. Will the peace hold? Will the 'centre hold' in the face of the immense demographic and societal changes now well underway?

FOOTNOTES

1. Tables 1 and 2, Population and Labour Force Projections, 1996-2026, Central Statistics Office, Dublin, April 1995.

2. Ibid.

3. Higher Education Authority: Report of the Steering Committee on the Future Development of Higher Education, Dublin, June 1995.

4. Population and Labour Force Projections, op cit.

5. Ibid, p 27.

6. FÁS/ESRI Manpower Studies: Occupational Employment Forecasts, 1998, Dublin, March 1995.

7. Table I, Higher Education Authority, op cit.

8. Annual Statistical Reports of the Department of Education, Dublin, *Irish Times* analysis (1995) for 1994 data.

9. Data produced by the Inter Parliamentary Union for Continental Europe.

David Kennedy

Strategic Trends

David Kennedy is a former chief executive officer of Aer Lingus, and former deputy governor of the Bank of Ireland. He is a director of a number of companies in Ireland and overseas and lectures in the Graduate School of Business in University College Dublin.

> *The future cannot be a continuation of the past,*
> *and there are signs ... that we have reached a point of*
> *historic crisis ... The structures of human*
> *societies themselves, including some*
> *of the social foundations of the capitalistic economy, are on the*
> *point of being destroyed by the erosion*
> *of what we have inherited from the human past.*
> *Our world risks both explosion an*
> *implosion – it must change.*
> AGE OF EXTREMES BY *EJ HOBSBAWM*

> *Things really have turned out far better than anyone*
> *looking at the world in 1950 could have reasonably*
> *expected. I believe that this general progress will continue.*
> *The fact that there are such intractable problems –*
> *of crime, drugs, family break-up, poverty and, in some parts of the*
> *world, hunger, danger and despair – should keep us humble.*
> *Provided we retain that*
> *humility there is no reason why the world in 2020*
> *should not be a still better place.*
> THE WORLD IN 2020 BY *HAMISH MCRAE*

When invited to contribute to this series of essays, my first selfish thought was to speculate whether I was likely to enjoy any personal experience of Irish business in 2020. I decided to consult with an actuary friend. Having consulted his book of tables he opined that my chance of survival until 2020 was about six to four on. It was hardly an overwhelming vote of confidence but enough to give me hope that I may have a personal stake in the outcome, whether it be the gloomy outturn predicted by Hobsbawm or the happier result foreseen by McRae.

I recently came across a series of forecasts made by a group of eminent US commentators in 1893 as to what life would be like in 1993. They predicted with great accuracy the advent of international aviation, television, widespread use of contraception and pollution controls. They were less accurate in forecasting the abolition of standing armies, life expectation of 150 years and substantial reductions in taxation!

This goes to show that while certain trends can be identified which are useful for forecasting purposes, nevertheless discontinuities and surprises are also a fact of life. In this century the ultimate discontinuity was World War I which led to the breakdown of Western civilisation of the nineteenth century. Such an event was not anticipated by these US forecasters and indeed the global political and social upheavals which it caused were beyond the expectation of any reasonable forecaster of the day.

In considering the outlook for Irish business in 2020, my approach has been to start by identifying current trends which can reasonably be projected forward, trends which have an impact on business such as those of a social, political, demographic, technological and environmental nature.

Having considered these trends, as well as some changes in the nature of business itself, I have tried to speculate as to what future events might trigger major discontinuities. All of this then comes together in an overview of Irish business by 2020 – hopefully one with perfect 20-20 vision!

SOCIAL TRENDS

In a number of respects the social foundations of our society are being increasingly threatened, both nationally and internationally. One obvious concern is the growth of organised crime internationally and the related growing problem of illicit drug abuse. In Ireland a serious drug problem is further compounded by the growing level of alcohol abuse by young people. A recent survey carried out in the Dublin area found that one-third of all under-eighteen-year-olds admitted to having been drunk over five times in their lives. Such excesses in alcohol consumption by young people could lead to increased levels of alcoholism in later life.

The stability of our society is also threatened by the increased incidence of marital breakdown and the growth in one-parent families. In the past the organised churches have provided moral leadership to Western civilisation, but today they are facing serious internal crises and their influence is accordingly weakened. High levels of unemployment and the growth of a non-work culture, particularly in urban areas, are compounding the risk that a two-tier society with a high incidence of crime will be a feature of life in Ireland in 2020.

On the other hand there are some positive social developments. Serious efforts are being made to improve the quality of our education and, perhaps even more importantly for social stability, its accessibility to deprived communities. Today the experience of foreign investors in Ireland suggests that they find the current products of our second- and third-level education system well up to international standards, although there is considerable scope for improvement in the teaching of science and mathematics.

Important changes are already taking place in the nature of work itself and these are likely to be accentuated in the years ahead. The traditional concept of a job for life is becoming outmoded. In future, people are likely to work for a number of employers throughout their working careers. There will be increased outsourcing of jobs, more part-time working, teleworking from home, contract piece working and, for older people, more voluntary work.

The short-term economic consequences of this more flexible labour market are positive but these may be offset in part by a diminution in the concept of company loyalty and pride which has been a feature of many successful societies, not least in Japan. A work ethic based exclusively on personal financial gain is neither attractive nor efficient. Not everyone would agree with Mrs Thatcher's dictum: 'There is no society, only individuals.'!

POLITICAL TRENDS

One would have to be brave to forecast political developments on the island of Ireland over the next twenty-five years. However, it does seem clear that from an economic perspective the Border will have become largely irrelevant. Provided that violence does not return, the potential exists for a substantial growth in trade between North and South to the mutual benefit of all parts of the island. The growth in business links should contribute to a reduction in the distrust and alienation that still exist. Reconciliation on the island may be an achievable objective.

On the international scene the probability is that the European Union (EU) will become wider but it may not become much deeper. There is limited public support across Europe at present for strengthening the current institutions and politicians will probably have to engage in a much greater degree of formal public consultation if they are not to lose touch with their constituents. Indeed the need for more public consultation may become an increasing feature of political life generally.

Developments within Europe will probably shift the centre of gravity in an eastward direction, leading to the reconstruction, firstly of Central Europe (Hungary, Czech Republic and Poland) and then of Eastern Europe. The immediate implications for Ireland are substantial reductions in transfer funds, both under the headings of Regional Development and the Common Agricultural Policy (CAP). On the positive side there will be increased markets for Irish exporters and a number of them have already turned their attention in this direction.

It is difficult to avoid a degree of scepticism about the feasibility of a single currency throughout the European Union, even by 2020. There are very few European currencies and economies today which could realistically contemplate coexistence with the Deutschemark. From an Irish perspective we will continue to live with the reality of an extremely close link with the British economy and our participation in a single European currency must depend very much on the future direction of British policy.

One other likely political development in Ireland and elsewhere is a diminution in the influence of national governments. This will occur in part because of the increasing influence of supranational organisations (such as the EU), in part because people increasingly wish for less government, and in part because of the globalisation of world trade and the power of international financial markets.

DEMOGRAPHIC TRENDS

Ireland is set to age considerably over the next twenty-five years. Although our ageing will be less dramatic than most of Western Europe, the projected changes are nonetheless quite dramatic. The Central Statistics Office (CSO) has projected that the number of people in the Republic of Ireland aged over sixty-five will increase by 40% between 1991 and 2021. In the same period the numbers aged between ten and twenty will fall by 26%. The World Bank has gone even further in its projections and for those who anticipate being around in 2050 they have projected a total of almost one million over sixty-fives in the Irish population by that time (an increase of 150% on the existing figure!).

This greying of our population has a number of implications. Health-care costs will rise, as medical costs rise steeply for people over sixty. The cost of providing for pensions will also be very considerable. In spite of current pressures for earlier retirement, people may have to stay at work longer since our tax system will not be able to cater for the combination of higher health and pension costs. Already in Florida, which has a high proportion of retired people, it is not unusual to see people in their seventies working part-time in supermarkets and other retail outlets. By 2020 an increasing proportion of our population will have to fund their own pensions, live on the proceeds of their savings and investments or continue in part-time work.

The recently published CSO Report on 'Population and Labour Force Projection' predicted decreased future participation rates in the labour force by people over fifty, reflecting a greater emphasis on early retirement. While this is consistent with current behaviour, it is doubtful whether society can afford to support increased numbers of older people on state pensions. What will probably happen is that the definition of labour-force participation will be less simple in the future as increased numbers of older people seek part-time work to supplement limited pensions.

There are other implications for business in this demographic shift. Older people have different needs and different consumption patterns and this will affect the demand for various products. For example, financial institutions will find that savings, investments and private pensions will be growth areas, whereas demands for credit and loans are likely to reduce. Older people are likely to constitute a vocal electoral pressure group which may force governments to adopt anti-inflationary policies so that the value of their savings will not be eroded. Older people have more time and often more interest in travelling so that tourism should continue to be a growth area in the future.

Whether an ageing population will compensate in increased maturity and stability for the loss of vitality and creativity that is associated with youth, is an open question. There must be some risk that Irish society collectively will be duller and more boring in 2020!

TECHNOLOGICAL TRENDS

The globalisation of business in recent years has owed much to technological improvements in transportation and communications. Looking forward over the next twenty-five years it is probable that improvements in transport will be at a more modest pace. However, in the communications industry, developments in micro-electronics and in software are fuelling major changes in existing products and also creating new products. Twenty-five years ago who would have anticipated the widespread use today of microwave ovens, video recorders, mobile telephones, walkman receivers, fax machines, compact discs and personal computers?

Much excitement has been generated about the 'global information highway'. I have reservations about certain aspects of this, in part because of a rather jaundiced view about the amount of rubbish currently transmitted on today's communications networks. Equally, the proposition that home shopping, using multimedia technology, will replace the regular visit to the supermarket or the local store seems to ignore the social aspects of today's shopping mode. Nevertheless, there will inevitably be developments on these lines. Mobile telephony will undoubtedly be a major growth area as will personal computers. Last year in the United States there were more personal computers sold than television sets and currently over 25% of US households use personal computers. In banking the use of Smart Cards is likely to eat into the use of paper money and of cheques but unlikely to overtake them within a twenty-five year time-frame.

If these assumptions about the growth of electronic products are correct then it follows that software development will also be a global growth industry. There are opportunities for Irish software firms but this is a highly mobile industry which could be carried out with equal facility in most parts of the world.

ENVIRONMENTAL TRENDS

In many respects we can anticipate a healthier and cleaner environment in 2020, with cleaner rivers, lakes and seas as well as cleaner air. In Ireland we are still only beginning to face up to our responsibilities to protect the environment and to avoid depleting our natural resources. In these matters we lag well behind most of Western Europe and the United States. This will mean added costs for some businesses but it will also offer a range of opportunities for businesses providing environmental services.

There is, of course, a danger in becoming too Green, aspiring to an imaginary idyllic non-industrial past. We can also note that there have been false alarms in the past when environmentalists frightened us with warnings that our natural resources were on the point of depletion. In 1970 the Club of Rome projected major crises by the turn of this century because of shortfalls in global food and energy resources. These projections seriously under-estimated both the impact of the Green revolution in improving agricultural productivity and the success of the oil industry in finding new fuel reserves.

Nevertheless, the real moral of the story about the little boy who cried wolf was that one day the wolf actually did arrive! The underlying message of the Club of Rome was that uninterrupted economic growth ultimately uses up natural resources and this message is still valid even if the time-scale of such depletion may be longer than originally expected.

There is also the issue of long-term environmental damage as a result of specific emissions. Action is already well in hand to cut back on CFCs and both NOx and SOx emissions. A more difficult issue is the question of CO_2, difficult because the scientific evidence about the greenhouse effect is far from conclusive and because the use of fossil fuels has become such an integral part of developed economies. However, the likelihood is that we will face some form of carbon tax early in the twenty-first century. This would have negative implications for peripheral economies such as Ireland because of its impact on transport costs.

Many parts of our national infrastructure should be in substantially better condition by 2020. Our roads and public transport will benefit from the heavy investment planned over the next ten years and it will be easier, safer and cheaper to travel round the country. Development of our major hospitals should be completed and market demand will have led to improved facilities for the care of elderly people.

GLOBAL ECONOMIC AND BUSINESS TRENDS

Any reasonable extrapolation of current trends would indicate that China will soon become the largest economy in the world. Any recent visitor to the Chinese mainland will have seen already the extraordinary dynamism of a people on the move. The expected growth of the Chinese economy should have very beneficial implications for the expansion of world trade. On the other hand, Japan may be the most powerful financial nation by 2020 with an enormous range of foreign investments (perhaps including increased ownership of Irish businesses).

In Ireland the importance of manufacturing is likely to diminish. In an increasingly global economy, more and more manufacturing will be carried out in those parts of the world which have low labour rates and/or very high productivity. Manufacturing processes for many products will shift to South-east Asia, Eastern Europe or Latin America where cost savings can be realised. A recently published estimate concluded that it costs as much today to employ one Japanese as 867 Russians!

As a result and also because of the continued impact of automation, the job trend in Irish manufacturing will be downwards. Although this has serious implications, it may be less disastrous than appears at first sight. Even today the manufacturing cost represents a small proportion of the total cost of bringing many products to the consumer. The principal costs often lie in adding value through design, packaging and distribution and, most importantly for global products, in brand development supported by multinational television advertising. These are areas in which Irish businesses can compete internationally.

Some of our existing manufacturing companies should be capable of survival in the global economy of 2020, if they can sustain their competitive advantages. The food and drinks sector which depends on our own natural resources is likely to remain internationally competitive. More recently established industries, such as the pharmaceutical and high-tech equipment sectors, have already developed deep roots in Ireland and accordingly are capable of forming independent and self-sufficient clusters.

Many Irish businesses will, of course, continue to depend primarily on the domestic market. The majority of small- and medium-sized Irish enterprises will be producing products which of their nature do not travel. Changes in world trade or technology will be less relevant for the purely domestic market (although in many instances that will be a thirty-two county market). However, increasing levels of competition and a low inflation environment will ensure that pressure on price margins is likely to be even more intense than today.

There are likely to be considerable changes in the ownership of Irish companies, but this will only be continuing the pattern of the past twenty-five years. A recent glance at the financial columns of the *Irish Times* in 1970 revealed frequent references to the following companies: United Distillers, McCairns Motors, Gouldings, PJ Carroll, The Hely Group, Dublin Artisans, Doreen, Cannocks, Tonge, Booth Poole, Pye (Ireland), Jacobs, Carrigaline Potteries, Glen Abbey and Irish Dunlop. Not one of these companies is currently quoted on today's Stock Exchange!

Increased trade in international financial services will ensure wider dispersion of ownership of Irish-based firms in twenty-five years' time. Even today our two largest industrial firms, Smurfits and CRH, have almost 40% of their shares held abroad. Perhaps by 2020 it will be commonplace for the interests of Japanese pension funds to be represented directly on the boards of prominent Irish companies! One could also speculate as to whether either or both of the two main Irish banks will have become part of a larger international grouping by 2020.

One welcome development should have taken place in Irish business, hopefully well before the year 2020, namely the withdrawal of direct government involvement in running commercial enterprises. Governments are not good shareholders, a fact which has been recognised almost universally outside of Ireland and there is no sensible reason for governments to continue to own hotels, banks and an airline.

UNFORESEEN DEVELOPMENTS

Much of the above is predicated on the basis that existing trend lines will continue. However, as we know, history does not run in straight lines. For example, one could speculate about the impact on world financial markets of a major earthquake in Tokyo or Los Angeles. What is the risk of a new plague or a major ecological disaster, such as a nuclear accident? Even worse, might we see the use of nuclear weapons, either in a local war or as part of a terrorist campaign? Political unrest in the former USSR could have serious implications for the rest of the world. The spread of Islamic fundamentalism through North Africa and into Europe is far from a remote possibility. Any such developments could lead to ethnic violence, social instability and economic downturns.

My own 'most likely' disaster scenario would be a replay, perhaps in a different form, of the energy crises of 1974 and 1980, each of which precipitated a global recession. An uncomfortably high proportion of the world's oil reserves is located in highly unstable political locations such as the Middle East and the former USSR. Uninterrupted energy supplies over the next twenty-five years would be a welcome but somewhat surprising outturn.

OVERVIEW OF IRISH BUSINESS IN 2020

What is the overall balance of forces likely to influence the shape of Irish business in 2020? As already outlined, these forces can broadly be categorised as either economic or social.

On balance, the economic outlook appears favourable. World trade is likely to continue to grow with the opening of new markets in Europe and elsewhere for Irish exporters. A member of Irish business sectors should be capable of competing effectively in international markets which have growth potential. These include food, drink, tourism, pharmaceuticals, high-tech equipment, professional services (financial, health, education, software, etc.) and artistic services (film, popular music, theatre). Employment in services will grow at the expense of manufacturing and hopefully our corporate tax system may shortly be realigned to encourage rather than discourage employment growth in the higher potential services sector.

On the other hand we appear to be facing a number of seriously disruptive social forces which threaten stability over the next twenty-five years. The incidence of organised crime and random crime appears to be on the increase throughout the developed world. The underlying reasons include growing alienation between haves and have-nots, the absence of effective moral leadership in an increasingly secular society, the breakdown of the traditional family unit and, very specifically, the growing drug culture.

More positively, we may hope to see increased reconciliation between the two communities on the island of Ireland and the growing business links between North and South can contribute to that process.

Our system of government in 2020 will probably still be struggling to find the correct balance between *laissez faire* and socialist ideologies, both of which have been tried and found wanting. Our welfare system will be under continual threat from rising healthcare and pension costs. The challenge will be as it is today, namely to encourage self-reliance and at the same time to provide a safety net for the weaker members of society.

It is tempting but probably futile to speculate on where the balance will lie between all of these conflicting forces in 2020. The reality is likely to be a complex combination of good and bad developments reflecting both the concern of Hobsbawm and the guarded optimism of McRae.

It is, however, important to remember that the future of Irish business will not be determined exclusively by the interplay of outside influences. 'The fault, dear Brutus, is not in our stars, but in ourselves, that we are underlings'! The position of Irish business in 2020 will ultimately be determined not by external forces but by the skills, the creativity and the hard work of our future business leaders. Perhaps more than any other group in Irish society, they will shape the future for the next generation.

Edward M Walsh

Evolving Universities [1]

Edward M Walsh is founding president of the University of
Limerick, founding chairman of both the National Techno-
logical Park, and the National Council for Curriculum and
Assessment.

GLOBAL BACKDROP

Since the first universities were established in Europe eight hundred years ago they have evolved slowly, yet steadily. Initially
they met the needs of a church-dominated society: teaching
theology, philosophy, medicine and law and producing priests,
doctors and lawyers.

The emergence of European colonial powers stimulated a
university response to the market-place by embracing the liberal
arts and focusing on the classics. Study of the ancient empires of
Greece and Rome was judged a fitting preparation for those who
would aspire to guide the emerging new empires of Europe.

The Industrial Revolution provoked a similar response and the
sciences were given emphasis. The foundation in 1834 of Hum-
boldt University in Berlin brought research activity formally
within the ambit of the university for the first time.

Only in the latter part of this century, with unprecedented
growth of global trade, have we seen business studies developed
as a major component of university activity.

Yet once more the university is responding to the market-place.
The emerging information age is stimulating a wide variety of new

courses and research within areas related to computer systems and informatics. High-powered information networks link universities and research laboratories in a new global network.

Unlike the preceding ages the new information age is of profound significance for the universities. Quite simply, knowledge, the strategic resource of the information age, is the commodity in which the universities have been dealing since their creation eight hundred years ago.

While the universities may have changed in response to the emerging colonial eras and the industrial eras, they still continued to exist on the fringes of society: enrolling considerably less than one in ten of the population until quite recently. Universities were nice adornments to society, but not crucial organisations controlling strategic resources essential to success in either the colonial or industrial eras.

Now all has changed. The spotlight has swung on the universities simply because they are now the providers of the key commodities crucial to success. Consequently, governments of nations large and small, combined with leaders of enterprise are now taking a special interest in the performance and standing of their universities: they recognise that the quality both of graduates and research will, to a considerable extent, determine their future competitiveness. Likewise, citizens in the developed, as well as developing, nations look to education, and especially the universities, as the best route towards success and a rewarding career.

In addition to the emergence of the information age a profound transformation in world history is stimulating a new social, economic and political order which will influence the shape of the Irish university and what happens within it. The collapse of communism has left most nations with only one choice: to join the market economy, in one way or another. John Meyer, professor of sociology at Stanford University highlights that 'improving education levels are creating a global middle-class that shares similar concepts of citizenship, similar ideas about economic progress and a similar picture of human rights'.

Against this global backdrop Europe may be poised for a new era of prosperity. Michael David-Well, senior partner of Lazard Freres & Co, predicts that Europe, east and west, will draw on its exceptionally well-educated population, new emerging entrepreneurial spirit and the fresh markets in Eastern Europe to break free of its slow-growth rut.

NATIONAL BACKDROP

If the David-Well prediction is correct, then Ireland is particularly well poised to respond. The world competitiveness report ranks the quality of Irish manpower amongst the world leaders.

	IRELAND	UNITED STATES	JAPAN
Availability of skilled labour	1	8	12
Availability of qualified engineers	1	13	17
Availability of competent senior managers	1	8	16
Economic literacy	2	16	1
Quality of life	3	10	19
Work motivation of young people	2	17	19
Attractiveness of engineering & science to young talented people	1	20	5
People have a positive attitude to life	1	7	5

Source: World Competitiveness Report, World Economic Forum, Geneva, 1993

In addition to its native population, the Irish diaspora represents a most exceptional global resource of talent and expertise which has the potential to transform this island both socially and economically. Assuming living standards continue to improve, and we have the courage to create an environment for enterprise, we can confidently expect to see the return of many thousands of well-educated, internationallyexperienced young people, attracted by our quality of life and the opportunity of becoming wealthy here in Ireland, while producing products and services for the global market.

IRISH UNIVERSITIES TO 2020

With this broad backdrop one can attempt to predict the future developments of the Irish university system.

Enrolment

Currently ninety thousand students are enrolled in Ireland's higher-educational system, of whom fifty-two thousand are enrolled in its universities.

While rapidly declining birth rates will begin to have effect on higher educational enrolments in this country, total enrolment will be determined primarily, not by birth rate, but by participation rates. This is reflected in Department of Education enrolment projections for the year 2005, showing a growth of 35% and university enrolment increasing by 44% to a total of seventy-five thousand.

The prospect of increasing university enrolment, despite falling birth rates, should not be a surprise; the phenomenon has been experienced in all developed countries. In Ireland, however, predicting enrolment has another special complication due to the presence of our diaspora. In the event that our economic and social circumstances combine to attract back increasing numbers of those who have emigrated (many with grown children), unpredictable and potentially large demand for additional places in higher education could be created.

Curriculum

The past twenty-five years has seen a spectacular increase in the choice of courses available to those going on to higher education. It can be expected that this trend will continue.

It can also be expected that the narrow academic base of many of the traditional programmes in areas such as law, engineering, arts and science will be broadened and enriched. On one hand it will be recognised that graduates in science and engineering will require more exposure to the arts and social sciences. It will be recognised that a traditional arts degree, which does not expose one to the sciences, provides, in this era, a narrow academic base indeed, and one which can be scarcely considered an adequate preparation for either life or work.

Examinations of the academic content of the traditional law degree, presented by most Irish universities, highlight the surprisingly narrow preparation provided for the profession. Models, found in the United States and Australia, where a broad base of preparation is provided at university prior to the study of law and other vocational programmes such as medicine, appear more appropriate.

Similar thoughts are emerging for those responsible for engineering education – with expectations that those who work in the sciences should be more aware of the environmental and social implications of their work.

Such pressures will lead to changes that will broaden and extend the traditional curricula in many disciplines.

Educational Technology

I recall when we were planning the first phase of development of what is now the University of Limerick, we were aware of the potential of the new educational technologies and of video recording in particular. It was suggested in the early seventies, when commercial video recording became economically viable that the best lecturers would be recorded and that the whole nature of teaching and instruction would change as a result.

Moved by this vision of the future we built not one, but two, television studios. However, we found that they lay unused for the most part and were ignored by the large majority of academics.

As educational technology has improved, so programmed learning, and programme-managed learning have arrived. These too have failed to capture the market. Now we have the prospect of multimedia systems to enrich and enliven the educational process. There appears to be little logic as to why such powerful education tools should not be widely adopted by both academic and student. However, if one recognises that a complete university education embraces much more than a few hours a day of lecture and tutorial, one can understand why. For the school-leaver who goes on to higher education, the three or four years of study for diploma or degree is as much about growing up, leaving one's home, establishing one's identity, making one's own decisions, forming new friendships, as about attending lectures and learning the content of the prescribed texts.

It is not too surprising therefore that the human interaction between student and faculty member, and between peers, which takes place in the live lecture theatre or seminar room or over a cup of coffee afterwards, cannot be replaced with fingers on a keyboard in front of a screen.

Like grand opera or ballet, undergraduate university education is likely to continue to a considerable extent in its present labour-intensive format: young people, in the process of leaving home, meeting and interacting with each other, learning and challenging convention, and at times making fools of themselves, will continue to need a place to congregate with large numbers of their like, while guided along the right path, to some extent at least, by their lecturers.

Educational technology will assist but not replace the lecturer.

Clearly the rapidly falling cost of data processing and communications makes it increasingly possible for every student to own or have access to all the computer power he or she needs. While not radically changing the undergraduate learning process, educational technology does promise to remove from both faculty member and student alike, some of the drudgery of teaching and learning. But the human, and at times somewhat primitive interaction between teacher and taught, and between students themselves which has characterised the learning process from earliest times, is likely to continue basically unchanged.

The constraints on library and data access are likely to be eased by the emerging capacity of computer systems to store and give access to data, relatively cheaply, on a global basis. Already major complete works can be carried around on CD. It is not unreasonable to expect that in some years students, when they enrol for a degree programme, will be able to purchase a CD, or its equivalent, containing copies of all the prescribed texts for the course and a lot of other relevant reading material. This is, of course, technologically feasible at present; the constraints are generally legal and economic. The Internet already makes access to world databases quite straightforward and facilitates research at locations remote from the world's great libraries.

Continuing Education

In the area of continuing education one can expect the most profound impact of technology. It is now well-recognised that one's primary qualification will require constant upgrading during one's career. Here educational technology will triumph. The mature person, anxious to upgrade a skill or acquire a new one, will much more readily sit and use a keyboard or multimedia programme either from home or work.

Continuing education will become a global commodity and

the concept of the Virtual University will become a reality for adults who wish to upgrade their qualifications or skills without greatly disrupting their existing home or work life.

The universities are presented with a major challenge in the field of continuing education. Irish universities with a base in the English-speaking world have potentially lucrative business opportunities in the development, operation and accreditation of multimedia continuing-education programmes for a global market.

VALUES

This century has seen the decline of the influence of the churches on society in the developed world. In recent decades a similar decline in the influence of the family is evident.

Voids have been created as a result.

Many would argue that the educational system should be called upon to play a greater role in filling such voids. More emphasis should be given to education of the whole person, as educators delve more deeply into the complex arena of values, ethics and social skills. In this century, educators have tended increasingly to limit their remit and concentrate on those areas where results can be readily quantified and judgements substantiated. However, it is now readily accepted that a surprising proportion of those who are proclaimed to be good and well-qualified by the educational system turn out otherwise. And conversely many who are now rejected as failures by the educational system, but who possess personal characteristics valued by society, such as integrity, enterprise, self-discipline, common sense, reliability, intuition, an ability to communicate, and prove honourable and trustworthy colleagues, fare remarkably well.

In the long run such values, which were once central to the educational process, count for more than a sterile knowledge of literature or science. Those universities that have the courage to challenge contemporary convention and give greater priority to developing in their students those prized human values, together with a high level of expertise in their field, are likely to be in the vanguard of success.

Management

At the turn of the century enrolment in the Irish universities could be measured in hundreds rather than in the thousands of today. The budgets of Irish universities now range from £30-£100 million a year and in the cities outside Dublin the universities are amongst the largest employers. With many campus companies, semi-autonomous research units and an extensive range of services, each university represents a complex organisation demanding both sophisticated structures and management skills.

Unfortunately the structures are often predetermined by outmoded legislative constraints which were enacted in another era and are often unsuited to today's needs. The universities in Ireland, as in the rest of Europe, have become enmeshed in state bureaucracy. At the turn of the century, there is no doubt that the world's greatest universities were in Europe. This can no longer be claimed: most of them are now to be found in the United States. Of the top ten, eight are private institutions, run with the same commitment to excellence and competitiveness which characterises the best of private enterprise.

Given the perceived importance of excellence in higher education for world competitiveness, it can be expected that university management structures, cost effectiveness of operations and quality of the product will be under increasing scrutiny as states look for relevance combined with cost effectiveness. The population at large demands value for money from its universities.

In this regard Irish universities are at a turning point. The prospect of removing fees, while generally welcomed by those who pay them, may have some undesired results, both social and economic, in the not too distant future. On one hand the 50% who do not go on to higher education (many of whom are underprivileged) will be expected, directly or indirectly, to subsidise those who do. While the universities, totally dependent on state support, are in danger of going the way of many totally subsidised state organisations: becoming bureaucratic, less vibrant, less responsive and less cost-effective.

There is no doubt that the state is wise to ensure that those who lack the means, and have the ability to benefit from higher education, gain access. However, if the state can afford to provide full support to all university students it might well consider paying these state subsidies directly to the students rather than directly to the universities: thereby ensuring that the universities are market-driven, even if by a proxy market. Indeed the future quality and standing of Irish universities may well hinge on the way in which the current decision is implemented. If, on one hand, the universities receive all their income directly from the state then there are sufficient models to examine to be fearful of a mediocre future at best. If, however, the students are directly subsidised, and the universities compete amongst themselves, then one could be more hopeful of ensuring dynamic, market-driven, entrepreneurial universities.

It is interesting to note that the emerging communist countries of central Europe, with some experience of what we plan, are now reviewing or altering the financing of higher education and reintroducing fees.

Communist China is at present doing likewise.

As in the case of car tax and rates on domestic homes which were removed in the past, university fees, or their equivalent, will gradually be reintroduced at some future period, amidst considerable anguish for all concerned.

Leadership

The great strides towards excellence of the best North American universities can be attributed to the quality of leadership at departmental, college and university levels. There, leadership is selected with the greatest care. Usually in Europe, university faculty members elect their leadership. However, in North America high-powered search committees are established when a key university position is being filled. Each university competes to attract prospective candidates and devotes considerable effort to the task.

In Europe things are otherwise – leadership is elected. While this might have made sense when one was dealing with a small community of scholars, with structures of an ecclesiastical kind, it makes little sense in an era of mass higher education, complex university systems and intricate management. Universities with electoral systems are noted for academic intrigue and the associated cliques.

Impending legislation for the Irish universities should ensure that a fresh start is made in arrangements for university leadership. The process of election should be replaced with a process of search and selection. Again, the future success and standing of the Irish universities will much depend on this point.

Globalisation

The ERASMUS programme of the European Union must surely be one of the most successful and cost-effective programmes devised by Brussels. As a result, thousands of students and many faculty members have moved between the European universities, building new friendships and cooperative relationships. These are underpinned by the powerful computer networks which interlink European universities and offer the prospect of ever-closer working relationships between like-minded institutions.

Just as a number of successful national businesses have

become global organisations, so it can be expected that success-ful national universities will form tightly-fused consortia with other universities and research institutions throughout the Euro-pean Union and internationally. In this way, linked together by computer networks and the mobility of students and faculty, new strong multinational university structures will emerge during the next twenty-five years. The effective mergers of universities across international lines will offer most students and researchers richer experiences than has been possible for all but a small minority in the past. Such multi-university groups will organise themselves in tight teams in the pursuit of prestige research contracts and of attracting the best students. The leading 'universities' in the next century are likely to be structured around such international consortia or university conglomerates.

University and Enterprise

As the needs of the information age progress it will be seen to be to the mutual advantage of both universities and enterprise to work more closely together. The physical manifestation of this is already evident with the creation of science and technology parks adjacent to, or in close proximity to, progressive universities throughout the world.

One can expect that the more successful universities will increasingly reduce the boundaries which distinguish them from the community and enterprise.

Already it is a common experience to find the most sophisti-cated scientific equipment in the laboratories of enterprise rather than within the universities. This will increasingly stimulate the incorporation of off-campus work as part of the undergraduate degree programme, while postgraduate qualifications at masters and doctorate level will be secured increasingly as a result of research conducted off-campus in the working environment and the laboratories of enterprise.

Integration of Higher Education

The distinction between universities and other colleges of higher education is likely to be eroded. Investment in the Regional Technical Colleges is being increased and it can be expected that the colleges will be designated under the Higher Education Authority. Over a period of years the Authority will then be likely to consider rationalisation in certain cases. Waterford Regional Technical College will evolve in the period towards university status. While in the case of cities such as Cork, Galway and Limerick it can be expected that closer working relationships will develop between the universities and the Regional Colleges. The government will be faced with the prospect of establishing two separate university-level institutions in each of these cities or integrating degree-level work within existing university structures.

International privatisation trends will have an influence in Ireland, and, if not seriously damaged by the removal of university fees, private sector colleges will emerge as important providers of higher education for special market segments.

Efforts to ensure that the Irish higher educational system is as dynamic and competitive as that of other countries, combined with world privatisation trends will lead to pressures to expose the universities to the reality of the market-place. Either a proxy market-place will be created, using a voucher system for fees, or the universities, through a privatisation process, will be exposed to the full rigours of the market. The state will continue to see well-educated citizens as a strategic resource and offer subsidies to the students directly and selectively.

CONCLUSION

All of the above is based on the naive assumption that individuals and society behave rationally and, consequently, predictably. However, history vividly demonstrates the fallacy of such an assumption.

Perhaps the only certainty, as one looks into the future, is that during the next twenty-five years the most unexpected scientific and social developments will take place, and some in positions of power will behave quite irrationally: thereby making our future as interesting as it is unpredictable.

FOOTNOTE

1. Originally presented as the McLaughlin Lecture at The Institution of Engineers in Ireland, 23 March 1995

Epilogue

Some of the threads running through these essays can now be woven into a tapestry depicting a composite, though somewhat blurred, vision of Ireland in 2020. The ideas, and the language of what follows, come almost exclusively from the contributors. I have merely sought to link them to present an overall picture.

GENERAL

The general outlook is optimistic. Indeed, the very first essay predicts that, in 2020, when account is taken of all the elements which accurately describe economic and social conditions, Ireland will have the highest quality of life in the world. At present, Ireland is in nineteenth position on the United Nations Index of Human Development.

Radical political ideas are put forward. One suggestion is that the organisation of government would be transformed. The Constitution of Ireland's Second Republic would provide for the direct election of a chief executive accountable to a smaller and more efficient House of the Oireachtas. Ministers would no longer be members of the Oireachtas but would be recruited from among those of proven experience and expertise in business, trade unions, and commercial life.

Others predict that the nation state itself will be subject to turbulence because of the ease of global communications. In fact, the changes wrought by global communications are a recurring theme. A Virtual World, it is forecast, will be brought about by the ease with which data, text, sound and images will be transmitted around the globe. So-called Virtual Communities will form among citizens of similar interests who will be as closely in touch as if they were living in the same neighbourhood.

As a result of these improvements in telecommunications, it is expected that increasing numbers of people would work from home, either as employees or as self-employed. Grasping the freedom offered by technology, individuals would choose to restructure their lives so as to improve their quality of life. Their employers would encourage them to do so as this work structure would prove to be more economical than providing office space in a single location.

Profound changes in the ethos and operation of business are expected as a result of the enhanced participation of women in the workforce. The crucial turning point is expected to be reached when women form a critical mass of about 30% in the higher echelons of organisations. This is described as a potential future shock!

Not all the social developments forecast are expected to be positive. The number of broken marriages is likely to increase. The rate of marriage breakdown in Ireland may increase significantly to the one in five level. However the current rate of marriage breakdown in the United States, one in two, is forecast to decline to one in five.

In addition, the number of people over the age of sixty-five will increase by 40% while the number between the age of ten and twenty will fall by 26%. This greying of the population will have significant implications for health-care costs as medical costs rise steeply for those over sixty.

SCIENCE, TECHNOLOGY AND TRADE

Next, the contributors assess the profound impact of science and technology. Science in its contribution to progress is nicely described as representing the eternal youth of the scientific mind. There is no doubt that in 2020, today's technologies, informatics, telecommunications, and biotechnology will be improved, but other technologies will hold the leading position. The technologies of 2020 are thought to be hidden among sciences such as the chemistry of molecular materials, nano-technologies, artificial intelligence, and mathematics, together with an understanding of the immune and nervous systems. The greatest break-throughs are expected when two or more technologies, emerging from different disciplines, come together. For example, in one such development it is speculated that Smart Glasses would be developed which would look like ordinary spectacles. However, they would combine a tiny microchip, with optics and holographic technology to enable the wearer to select and obtain information by voice activation from a broadcasting network and to observe the response on the upper part of the spectacle lens. It is also speculated that greater understanding of the human immune system would lead to cures for AIDS and various genetic disorders. None can foresee with any precision the discoveries that will be made or the technologies to which they will give rise. The only certainty is that they will surprise us.

In another bullish forecast it is suggested that research and development expenditure in Ireland would be the highest in Europe, but even then would lag behind that of China. Government would be far more technologically-driven than at present, similar in fact to that of rapidly-growing Singapore today where the majority of top civil servants and a high proportion of politicians are technologists.

Major changes are also expected in international trade. The freeing of world trade through the activities of the World Trade Organisation (WTO) will probably lead to the development and manufacture of products for new markets at a breathtaking pace. The positive impact of greater demand from a more prosperous China and India would more than off-set the disruption caused by rapid change. However, a warning note is sounded – the

European Union will have a multi-tiered system of regulations, while its competitors in the United States and the Pacific Rim will be governed by a simpler structure established by the World Trade Organisation.

VIRTUAL REALITY

And so we come back to one of the dominant themes running through these essays – the Virtual World. Virtual Reality and its impact on behavioural patterns is explored from many points of view. New technologies, even now, provide the viewer with direct access to visual images and the spoken word, and these images can be commanded, controlled and interacted with. Composers can transmit music, not just notes on paper; artists can transmit pictures, not just ideas in words; and educators can provide children with something very close to real experiences without the effort of decoding print and harnessing imagination.

These possibilities, it is believed, will lead to the formation of the Virtual Communities across international boundaries, mentioned above, including the opportunity to create a network out of the Irish diaspora. Such Virtual Communities would reduce the need to travel. However, lest we get carried away by our perceptions of this new world, we are reminded that whether it is watching the sun set on a Connemara bog or the sun rise on the Nile it is not expected that Virtual Reality would replace personal experience.

ARTS AND CULTURE

The appeal of scenery to the senses leads us on to an assessment of the future for what we now call the 'cultural industries'. These industries, comprising the performing arts, media, visual arts and design heritage and libraries, are set to expand sharply. Already they employ as many as the banking sector, while Arts Council expenditure has increased over the last twenty-five years by twelve times in real terms.

Technology, such as the ubiquitous Virtual Reality, will offer novel forms of experience, changing the form or means by which art is experienced and the interaction between audience and artist. But it is unlikely that these new art forms or ways of experiencing would *replace* existing ones, rather they would form new niche markets. The actual presence of pictures, of actors, of musicians, etc, and the often public and collective nature of the transactions between them and their audiences, are profoundly *social* events.

From another perspective it is asserted that Ireland should not, indeed cannot, reject the new era of communications, but should instead develop and protect its own culture and identity. An awareness of cultural difference could then increase appreciation of Ireland's heritage and traditions and continue to make the Irish unique.

INDUSTRIAL RESTRUCTURING

Industry, as usually defined, can also expect dramatic developments. A number of factors – globalisation of production, the decline of the nation state, the rise of the individual, the greening of politics and the increasing speed with which new products become redundant – will produce new pressures which may force us to alter our relationship with the environment and to rediscover community and the unique value of personal relationships. Organisations may then increasingly fade away yielding to networks of relationships which are immediately and profoundly supportive.

The Virtual World of the future is expected to be realised well in advance of the year 2020. It would require early access to a Broad Band Global Telecommunications Network. Its projected impact on manufacturing would be the most potent factor in eliminating the actual or perceived peripherality of Ireland. The operation and control of remote manufacturing processes, located to suit raw material supply and markets, could then be conducted from Ireland. Furthermore, it is regarded as highly likely that most Irish multinationals of the future will operate in the world of services rather than in manufacturing.

In contrast, another essayist predicts that the successful company of the future would be the one employing a relatively small number of people who concentrate on a few key skills, and that the rate of growth and decline of companies will become much more rapid. This implies the need for companies to become clusters of units, concentrating on related but different tasks. In this new world, companies then take on a modular form. Consequently, they will need to combine strategically with other companies possessing complementary skills.

On balance, the outlook is regarded as particularly favourable for many sectors of Irish business, including food, drink, tourism, pharmaceuticals, high-tech equipment, professional services (financial, health, education, software, etc) and artistic services (films, popular music, theatre).

Nor should we ignore the political and economic changes now underway on this island. It is perceived that the business traditions and strengths of Northern Ireland are very different to those of the Republic. Greater business links and synergy between the business sectors on the island would release a considerable economic dynamic. Both North and South have highly professional investment promotion agencies and working together to attract and develop investment would bring mutual benefits.

AGRIBUSINESS

Agriculture has always been a primary concern of the Irish people. Here, too, substantial changes are forecast. World growth in agricultural output, will continue to slacken. The rate of growth in agricultural output, which was 2.4% per annum in the 1970s, is forecast to fall to 1.8% over the next twenty years. Already China has been unable to supply North Korea with grain. The United States has stepped in to fill the breach, and all setaside land has been scrapped. World population is forecast to reach 8.3 billion by 2025 compared with over 5 billion today.

Who will produce the food of the future? On the one hand, China has 22% of the world's population but only 7% of the arable land, on the other, there are greatly under-utilised agricultural resources in Africa, South America and Eastern Europe.

There is a provocative prediction of the impending demise of supply-side management policies alongside concern that Europe will remain overly bureaucratic. The supply-side management of food production in the European Union is frustrating the advances of technology at farm level, and resulting in the surrender of markets to the United States, Australia and New Zealand.

On a more positive note, it is envisaged that Irish agribusiness will have established a network of supply depots and infrastructure facilities across Europe by 2020. These firms will contract with Irish farmers for the supply of a standard beef product all year round. The future of the Irish beef industry is considered to be assured, because of the ease with which weight is gained while animals are on grass.

CONSTRUCTION

Some industries are expected to remain the same. Construction products will probably not change dramatically. The industry will continue to reshape the products of earth, such as concrete, clay products, glass, timber, aluminium, etc, as it always did. However, products will be extracted with more care for the environment, and land will be restored in an attractive and properly landscaped manner. The products will be made with less energy and waste, and will be recycled where this can be done economically.

Happily, buildings are expected to be more aesthetically pleasing and more in conformity with their natural surroundings. It is hoped that they will be energy efficient, quiet and healthy and designed to allow for change. Roads will be quieter, cars will be more energy efficient and safer, and towns and cities will again become pleasant for the pedestrian and cyclist. People should have enough individual space to satisfy their needs, and the liberty and capacity to create their own immediate environment.

TRANSPORT AND ENERGY

At one end of the spectrum there is the view that policies of limitation on the growth of cities, and the continuing shift of populations from cities to smaller urban and rural locations, will alter attitudes to transport. The Information Superhighway will encourage relocation, and working from home will become the norm for many who prefer to live and work away from 'the madding crowd'.

At the other end of the spectrum, it is predicted that the development of hypersonic commercial aircraft will enable planes carrying five hundred people to travel via near outer space from Frankfurt to Sydney in four hours. The world, already a global information village, will by 2020 have become a physical village.

In the field of energy, international pressures will force action to combat the greenhouse effect and the diminution of the ozone layer. Ireland will be bound by international protocols to reduce carbon dioxide and sulphur dioxide emissions progressively.

TOURISM

In addition, a major improvement in the preservation of the environment in Ireland seems certain. This will embrace the water quality of the seas and estuaries, the preservation and enhancement of the landscape, town and village planning, and the enhanced availability of information on cultural sites.

The number of overseas visitors to Ireland almost trebled over the past twenty-five years, and has shown a growth rate of 7% per annum since 1985. Ireland is currently increasing its share of the European tourism market. This rate of growth is expected to continue into the next century. Although now a long way off saturation, it will be necessary to come to terms with maintaining a sustainable volume of visitors. Advances in information technology will change the *need* to travel to the *option* of travelling. This will create a demand to provide the visitor with a richer experience than in the past.

Travel and tourism are predicted to be the world's greatest industry long before the year 2020. An increasing amount of the wealth generated by tourism will be goal directed. People will use their breaks to do, discover and explore. The idea of a holiday with the sole purpose of relaxation is well on the way to extinction. Cultural tourism, for which Ireland is superbly placed, is a long way from the superficiality of traditional sight-seeing.

RETAILING

Lifestyles are expected to change as consumers alter their shopping habits. By 2020 the customer should be able to demand products and services from the manufacturing/distribution complex that correspond more closely to their individual needs. Shopping everywhere is likely to be unrestricted by law and opening hours to be determined by customer demand. This will mean stores are open twenty-four hours, seven days a week.

Despite this not everyone will go to the store to do their shopping. For some products, home shopping may become the norm as soon as the technology can be made user-friendly enough. For others, home delivery will come into its own again, as was the case with pizzas. This is just the tiny tip of a massive future business. For yet other products customers may be offered economies of scale if they buy certain goods at less frequent intervals.

It is predicted that the worlds of leisure, eating and shopping may become totally intertwined. Local tastes and preferences will never be totally subdued. In the US today the market leaders in retailing operations are invariably regional operations not national ones. This suggests that closeness to the customer is essential to successful retailing. However, for some products the whole of Europe may become one market-place with telephone ordering and overnight delivery common occurrences.

FINANCIAL SERVICES

The way we conduct our financial affairs is also likely to be quite different. Much of the personal contact between customers and their banks is expected to be carried on from the home. Interactive video would link the user to their bank manager via secure Cable TV on powerful personal computers.

Furthermore, within financial services generally customers would require service relating to the movement of money, protection against risk, savings, pensions and loans. For each of these, customers would want to choose their own required product from a series of modular choices. This means that customers will demand access to systems which enable them to make such choices.

While information on all our transactions may be totally available to us in our houses, 2020 will not see a brave new world of people sitting at home conducting their affairs with no social contact. The need for both social contact and for advice through the maze of available information will probably become greater rather than less.

UNIVERSITIES

Like grand opera or ballet, undergraduate university education is likely to continue – to a considerable extent – in its present labour-intensive format: young people in the process of leaving home, meeting and interacting with each other, learning and challenging convention, will continue to need a place to congregate with large numbers of their peers, while being guided along the right path, to some extent at least, by their lecturers. Education technology, it is forecast, will assist but not replace the lecturer.

However, education is likely to become more international. Continuing education will become a global commodity and the concept of the Virtual University will become a reality for adults who wish to upgrade their qualifications or skills without greatly disrupting their existing home or work life.

Successful national universities would be the ones which form tightly-fused consortia with other universities and research institutions throughout the EU and internationally. In this way, linked by computer networks and the mobility of students and faculty, new strong multinational university structures will emerge during the next twenty-five years.

On an encouraging note, it is suggested that Irish universities, which attracted less than £50 million in research grants in 1993, might receive £1 billion for this purpose in 2020.

UNFORESEEN DEVELOPMENTS

The general thrust of the above forecasts is very positive. However, some political threats are identified.

One extreme speculation is that there will be a middle-class tax revolt throughout Europe. In this scenario the European government would take all value-added tax generated throughout the EU, leaving national government responsibility only for education, law and order and social welfare. Middle-class areas of major cities would begin to use the money, which would once have been paid in income tax, to develop their own secure areas.

Perhaps a more likely disaster scenario would be a replay of the energy crises of 1974 and 1980, each of which precipitated a global recession. An uncomfortably high proportion of the world's oil reserves is located in highly unstable political locations such as the Middle East and the former USSR. The spread of Islamic fundamentalism through North Africa and into Europe is far from being a remote possibility. The impact on world financial markets of a major natural disaster, such as an earthquake, could also be enormous.

IRELAND AS A MODEL

To revert to the optimistic tone that runs through these essays – it is forecast that Ireland will become a campus of excellence, a model society that will be the envy of larger nations. This process would be greatly facilitated by the small size of our nation. The traditions and cultural cohesiveness which result from Ireland's geographical isolation would be its strength; while the input from foreign cultures fed back from the Irish diaspora would provide the impulse for a more outgoing attitude to the world at large.

Consistent with the earlier view that Ireland may have the highest quality of life in the world, it is predicted that Dublin will be a world-class city, an 'intelligent' city that has harnessed new technology to allow transport, public services, telecommunications, shopping and other key services to respond rapidly to the needs and desires of the inhabitants. Tourists from Munich to Milan would bring the streets alive. There would be a National Convention Centre and the city might even have hosted the European Games and the Olympic Games. A city of low unemployment and high quality jobs, Dublin would be one of Europe's leading centres of knowledge-based industries.

CONCLUSION

These essays have presented a vision of 2020 which can still only be seen in part through a glass darkly, and yet there are flashes of brilliant clarity. Many contributors have taken risks in order to stimulate the imagination of the reader. Others have sought to deepen our understanding of the processes in train.

The dominant mood is one of confidence and optimism that the Ireland of 2020 will be a more exciting place in which to live, that it will have the capacity and willingness to embrace enthusiastically the rapid changes in technology as a tool of mankind, and that human and social relationships will remain as important as ever.

Other Books from

 O'BRIEN BUSINESS

CROWNING THE CUSTOMER
How to become Customer-Driven
Feargal Quinn

The bestselling hands-on guide to running a customer-focused business.
From an internationally acclaimed entrepreneur.
£6.95 pb
'A manual for all businessmen'
STUBBS BUSINESS GAZETTE

UP THE LOYALTY LADDER
How to make your Customer your best Promoter
Murray & Neil Raphel

A practical business strategy for turning prospective shoppers into loyal
customers, and ultimately the best promoters of your business. From one
of the world's leading marketing gurus.
£11.99 pb
'One of the best business books of the year'
SOUNDVIEW EXECUTIVE BOOK SUMMARIES

ORDER FORM

These books are available from your local bookseller. In case of difficulty order direct from
THE O'BRIEN PRESS.

Please send me the books as marked. I enclose cheque / postal order for £......... (+ 50p
P&P per title) OR please charge my credit card ☐ Access / Mastercard ☐ Visa

Card number ☐☐☐☐ ☐☐☐☐ ☐☐☐☐ ☐☐☐☐

EXPIRY DATE ☐ ☐ ☐ ☐

Name: ....Tel: ....

Address:..

Please send orders to: THE O'BRIEN PRESS, 20 Victoria Road, Dublin 6.
Tel: (Dublin) 4923333 Fax: (Dublin) 4922777